:60 SECOND
ANGER MANAGEMENT

:60 SECOND
ANGER MANAGEMENT

Quick Tips to Handle
Explosive Feelings

Dr. Michael Hershorn

New Horizon Press
Far Hills, New Jersey

152.47
Her

Hershorn, Michael
    :60 Second Anger Management: Quick Tips to Handle Explosive Feelings

Cover Design: Norma Erler Rahn
Interior Design: Susan M. Sanderson

Library of Congress Control Number: 2001090027

ISBN: 0-88282-220-9
New Horizon Press

Manufactured in the U.S.A.

2006   2005   2004   2003   /   5   4   3   2

This book is dedicated to

Alexandra Kate Hershorn
&
Zackary Ross Hershorn

To paraphrase Billy Joel's "Lullabye":
Goodnight, my angels
Now it's time to dream
And dream how wonderful your lives will be

AUTHOR'S NOTE

The material in this book is intended to provide a quick overview of methods and information now available. Any of the treatments described herein to manage or control anger should be discussed with a licensed health care/mental health practitioner. The author and publisher assume no responsibility for any adverse outcomes which derive from the use of any of these treatments in a program of self-care or under the care of a licensed practitioner.

The information in this book is based on Michael Hershorn's research and practices. Fictitious identities and names have been given to characters in this book. Some of the characters in this book are composites of patients who participated in the author's research studies. For the purposes of simplifying usage, the pronouns he and she are often used interchangeably.

TABLE OF CONTENTS

INTRODUCTION

Congratulations. Whether you are reading this book out of your own choice or due to the influence of someone else, you have taken an important step toward dealing with your anger management problems. There is a useful saying in the self-help support group movement that applies well here. It is: "Bring the body and the mind will follow." I say to you: "Bring the mind so that the body will follow." By reading this book and practicing the exercises, your behavior, thinking and feelings will change and you will benefit from it. You will learn to manage your anger in positive, healthy ways. You are not alone.

In *:60 Second Anger Management* you will read actual case histories of people I have helped in my practice, to reinforce that you are not alone, to make the information come to life and to foster positive expectations of change. Undoubtedly, many of you will find aspects of your own experiences being described and will relate to the individuals in the case examples. The names and other minor descriptive characteristics have been changed to protect the confidentiality of my patients. I have written about them with their knowledge and permission. All of these people are enthusiastic about having their stories told. They feel good that others will be helped. This is often common in the process of change. First people work on themselves and then when they can help someone else, they do, because it helps cement their own changes even further. People come full circle; from anger, guilt, shame and remorse to overwhelming feelings of relief and well-being, as well as a desire to share their successes and help others.

Let me take :60 Seconds to tell you something about myself. I have worked in the mental health field since 1978 and I have been a psychologist since 1984. As a clinical psychologist I have worked for the New York City Police Department, Psychological Services Unit and Alcohol Counseling Unit, at the Broward Sheriff's Office, Behavioral Sciences

Unit and I have been a faculty member and clinical director at the American College of Advanced Practice Psychologists. I have also been in private practice since 1984 and established my own full-time group practice in 1991. I am currently a Captain in the United States Army Reserve, Medical Service Corps. Since graduate school I have specialized in the research and treatment of anger management problems. My Masters thesis research focused on the effects on children growing up in homes where they witnessed marital conflict and marital violence. My doctoral dissertation research focused on defining subtypes of those who engaged in spouse abuse. I demonstrated that there are at least two types with different forms and frequencies of violence and different backgrounds. These are "over-controlled hostile" versus "under-controlled hostile" individuals.

My research has resulted in presentations at annual conventions of the American Psychological Association and articles in professional journals. I have also published a number of articles on other psychological subjects in professional journals. My research has been funded by both private foundations and the federal government through the National Institute of Mental Health.

In addition to my research, I have been treating people with anger problems since 1980, leading workshops for groups and working one-on-one with individuals with anger management problems. This work has been the springboard for my research and writing. I have learned a great deal about anger problems from working with and counseling people and this has directed my scientific investigations into anger problems and their impact on men, women, children, marriages and families. My time spent helping people who have anger problems has been the most rewarding work of my career.

When I first started, many therapists were afraid to work with people who had anger problems. Over time, we came to understand that people with mismanaged anger are not dangerous, nor bad, nor monsters. They are simply people who have learned to express their anger in unhealthy ways. Individuals who sought help often thought of themselves in the same negative ways others did. With therapy and counseling, they discovered they were not alone, their behavior could be understood and they could learn to change. My approach as a psychologist, working with people with all types of problems, has never been to judge, only to understand. So let's embark on a journey together. Let's figure this thing out as a team. Let's work and achieve success together.

Be honest, open up to yourself and do not be judgmental. Understand that there are reasons your difficulties with anger have developed and there are solutions. Discover that the success rates are very high and in your favor.

:60 Second Tips: Anger Management Introduction

♦ Bring the mind so that the body will follow.

♦ You are not alone.

♦ You will not be judged.

♦ Anger problems are learned and can be unlearned.

♦ The case histories you will read will be helpful in reassuring you that others have similar problems.

♦ Do the exercises. Practice the skills.

♦ I am with you and on your side.

♦ The success rates are high and it is likely that you will learn to deal with anger more effectively.

PART I

ABOUT ANGER

"How much more grievous are the consequences of anger than the causes of it."
-Marcus Aurelius

CHAPTER 1

How to Manage Your Anger in :60 Seconds

*"Without change, something sleeps inside us, and
seldom awakens. The sleeper must awaken."*
-Frank Herbert

Anger is a normal emotion. Problems come about depending on what we do with our anger. Any expression other than talking about our anger is acting on our anger and can be destructive to others and ourselves. Our ultimate goal is to learn to express our feelings of anger calmly in words. Many of us have learned ineffective ways of expressing our anger. These habits can be unlearned. This book will help you to manage your anger more constructively within the first :60 Seconds of becoming angry. With practice you will achieve our ultimate goal of expressing anger calmly in words and in just :60 Seconds. The benefits will include feeling more understood, being able to quickly resolve conflicts and feeling better about yourself.

C.A.R.E.: Four Steps to :60 Second Anger Management

You can learn to **C.A.R.E. C.A.R.E.** refers to the four steps engaging the right technique for achieving anger management in :60 Seconds. They are:

1) **C**ommitment to change
2) **A**wareness of your early warning signs
3) **R**elaxation
4) **E**xercising self-control with Time Outs

Learning the acrostic **C.A.R.E.** will help you to remember the four steps to :60 Second anger management. Let's take an in-depth look at each of the four steps individually.

"C" is for <u>C</u>ommitment to change. By reading this book you have already made a commitment to change. If someone has strongly suggested you read this book, make the best of it. As long as you are reading it, you may as well have a positive attitude and be open to change. Then no one will ever tell you to do something about your anger again. In working with people who have had anger management problems, the first step is asking them to make a commitment to change. State a commitment to yourself now. Write it down. Paste it to your bathroom mirror. This takes only :60 Seconds.

_____

_____

_____

_____

We will go over case histories in this book to give you something real with which to relate. You may read about a person in a case history and say, "Hey, that sounds just like me!" Later we will hear about Dennis. He came to me for help, but he had already made the commitment never to act out on his anger toward his wife in a destructive way again. He was on the verge of losing his wife, his children, his home, his money and the respect of his family and friends. He was committed to managing his anger and that was half the battle. Of course, change is more complicated than just making a commitment to do it. How many people have made commitments, like New Year's resolutions to stop smoking or lose weight, only to fail? Dennis was committed and that was good. It kept him coming for help even when it was inconvenient or when there were seemingly more important things to do. The skills he learned in treatment helped him to keep his commitment.

Allow your commitment to keep you reading this book even when it is inconvenient or there are other activities you'd rather do or you feel you ought to do. Allow your commitment to motivate you to do the exercises included in this book. Doing the exercises means just that. Do not just skim over them and say to yourself, *Oh, I got the idea. I don't actually have to do that.* We are trying to change behaviors and habits that have been learned long ago, repeated for years and even reinforced. We must practice new ways of acting and thinking in order to change. Besides, many of the exercises will only take :60 Seconds. The others will become second nature and frequent practice will give you many :60 Second anger management tools.

"A" is for <u>A</u>wareness of your anger cues, signs or signals. People say many things when they act out destructively on anger: *I just snap... I lose control... I just go off... I totally lose it.* Think about yourself. When you "went off on your boss" or "lost it with your co-worker," did you...

- Tackle him to the ground and start pummeling?
- Tear her office apart?
- Scream at the top of your lungs?
- Use the foulest language possible?

If you ever hit your spouse, girlfriend or boyfriend, did you...

- Hit him as hard as you possibly could?
- Use a clenched fist as opposed to an open hand?
- Choose to hit in the face instead of a less damaging place like the shoulder?

If you were enraged by a cop for pulling you over, did you...

- Physically attack her?
- Go for his gun?
- Threaten her life or try to harm her?
- Ram your car into his?
- Refuse to give her your license, registration or insurance?

When someone cut you off on the road, did you...

- Smash his car with yours?
- Follow her to her destination and fight with her or trash her car?
- Run him off the road or smash his windshield with a baseball bat?

In my experience as a therapist, the answers to these questions have invariably been "NO." In other words, we may act destructively on our anger but not in the most <u>extreme</u> way. You still need to learn management skills, but it is not true that you lose <u>complete</u> control. You are exerting some control even when acting out on your anger. This is good news. If you are already practicing some form of control, you can learn to continue maintaining that level of control and work to further increase your self-control.

Since you really are in control, you can learn to recognize the signs that you are becoming angry almost immediately. You do not just "go off" or "snap." There are early warning signs. These signs can be emotional (feeling angry), behavioral (actions), physiological (sensations) and cognitive (thoughts). Since the emotional signal—feeling angry—is difficult to identify at first, let's focus for now on the other three types of warning signs.

Physiological cues or sensations can include:

· Face flushing
· Quickened heart beat
· Heart pounding
· The feeling of blood rushing though your veins
· Feeling hot
· Muscles tensing

Behavioral cues or actions can include:

· Pacing
· Restlessness
· Inability to sit still
· Clenching of fists or jaw
· Talking more rapidly or loudly
· Punching one's hand
· Stomping

Cognitive cues or thoughts can include:

· *He's doing this purposely to make me explode.*
· *This has been a bad weekend. Now I would just love to explode.*
· *This is not acceptable.*
· *She is intentionally trying to make a fool of me.*

These are examples of all the types of early warning signs that anger is building. With them, you are alerted that you might react with a destructive expression of anger. Take :60 Seconds and write down your own usual early warning signs of anger. This will help you to remember them and recognize them. You will eventually be able to recognize your early warning signs of anger in :60 Seconds or less. With this knowledge, you can decide to act differently.

_____

_____

_____

_____

"R" is for the <u>R</u>elaxation Response. This has to do with acting on your anger differently. The state of relaxation is antithetical to anger. If you are relaxed, you cannot possibly be angry. It is neurologically and physiologically impossible. Once you have recognized a sign or two of anger, you can activate relaxation. The earlier you intervene, the easier it is to shift from anger to relaxation. Many people already use relaxation methods even if just to unwind after a long day. If you are one of them, you can use these same methods to head off acting out on anger. Such relaxing activities may include taking a walk, bicycling, taking a shower or bath, lying down, picking up a book or magazine, watching television, listening to music, breathing deeply, practicing yoga, praying or meditating. You can choose to use your relaxing activities to head off anger. It is important to focus on the relaxation and not brood about what made you angry. Our goals are to get the mind to stop dwelling on the anger and get the body relaxed.

There are some quick relaxation techniques that you can use to calm down in :60 Seconds. Different techniques work for different people, so experiment. Or you can mix and match techniques that work for you. Get yourself into either a sitting or lying down position in which you are using as few muscles as possible to hold yourself in that position. Breathe in though your nose and out through your mouth. As you breathe in say *calm* to yourself and as you breathe out say *peace* to yourself. Do this rhythmically in tune with your breathing.

Another method for controlling your emotions is to focus on muscle tension. Notice if there is tension in any of the major muscle groups of your body and relax it away, going from the top of your head to the tips of your toes. Imagine draining the tension down and out of your body. Or imagine that the chair or bed you are resting on or the wall you are leaning against is like a big sponge absorbing the tension out of your body. The major muscle groups are those in your head and face, your neck, your shoulders, your arms, hands and fingers, your chest, your stomach, your upper and lower back, your butt and thighs, your calves and your feet and toes. Check each part of your body and release any tension and relax the muscles. Notice the difference between the bad feelings of tension and the good feelings of relaxation. Remember to go from the top of your head to the tips of your toes.

A third, more active method of using relaxation to manage anger is to do the same as just described, but first purposely tense the muscles in each major group for three counts and then relax them for five counts. You will begin to notice the tension as it builds, as you tighten the muscle and hold it. Then you will notice the tension drain away as you release and relax your muscles. This exercise will train you to become more quickly aware of muscle tension. The quicker you notice it, the easier it will be to relax it away. We all walk around during the day with varying degrees of muscle tension and do not even realize it. Many of us hold tension in particular places like the neck and shoulders. By being aware and relaxing tension away each time it is noticed, you reduce stress and become less likely to feel irritated or become angry. You can increase your sense of calm and well-being, because as we relax on the outside we relax on the inside as well.

It is said that a picture is worth a thousand words. This saying can be applied to anger management. Another relaxation technique to help you master your anger involves the use of imagery. Close your eyes and put yourself, in every sense, in a real place where you have felt relaxed and at peace. Utilize all of your senses. For example, imagine yourself lying on a sandy beach. Feel the sand beneath the blanket perfectly cradling your body. Feel the warm sun on your skin and a cooling breeze brush over you, keeping the balance between hot and cold perfect. Hear the sounds of the waves rolling into shore, the wind as it rustles through the dune grass and the seagulls' muted cries in the distance. See the blue sky, some white puffy clouds and the gulls circling high overhead. See the long expanse of white beach and the waves breaking into white foam on the shore. Look to the horizon and notice that fine line where the ocean meets the sky. See the difference between the blue-green of the ocean and the blue of the sky. Smell the briny sea air as you slowly breathe in and breathe out. The air is so vibrant you can almost taste the freshness and saltiness. Place yourself in a relaxing scene such as this in every sense. See, feel, hear, smell and even taste it. This is a place to which you can return whenever you need to and whenever you want to. It is like taking a mini-vacation during the course of the day. This will keep your general level of tension down. Use it when you notice anger cues and put yourself in that special place as fully as possible. The more you practice, the easier it will become and the more motivated you will be to use this relaxation technique.

Another technique you can use for controlling anger is to make suggestions to yourself. When you are relaxed, you become more receptive and open. This is like self-hypnosis, which is nothing more than getting relaxed and making positive suggestions to yourself. For example, you might say to yourself when relaxed, *I will let my anger go; I will focus on what is good and not what is bad; I will express my anger in words; I will practice relaxation exercises as soon as I notice anger signs.*

You have now learned several techniques to use as tools to reduce anger. You can now break the vicious cycle of feeling then acting on your anger by substituting it with relaxation methods. Each of these techniques can be practiced or used in :60 Seconds.

"E" is for Exercising Self-control. This involves taking a Time Out from a situation that is generating the normal human emotion we call anger. By removing yourself from an angry situation, you give yourself the chance to calm down now and come back to it later, when you are able to deal with it in a more constructive way. More than one Time Out may be needed in a situation. As anger cues are noticed, it is okay to announce the need for a Time Out and walk away to avoid acting out on anger in a destructive manner. During the Time Out, a relaxation technique should be used. Return to the situation as soon as you are calm enough to address any problems or conflicts with the other person. This way he or she will not feel avoided, "blown off" or shut out by the Time Out technique and will trust it in the future.

It might not be appropriate to tell a boss, teacher, co-worker, friend or police officer that you need to take a Time Out for a while. These are times when you can simply announce a Time Out to yourself in your head. Use the imagery technique to go to a relaxing place and practice a relaxation skill like rhythmic breathing while repeating the words *calm* and *peace* to yourself.

In a relationship with a significant other, explain the Time Out technique ahead of time when emotions are calm. This is so the concept is fully understood by the other person and will most likely be followed in the heat of an angry moment. Either party may call a Time Out. The Time Out is always called for yourself, not for the other person. Ultimately, you only have control over yourself. If you tell someone else to take a Time Out, he or she may resist being told or ordered to do something and may feel controlled. The Time Out will then become the focus of the argument. Each person takes responsibility for noticing his or her own anger and for calling his or her own Time Out. That person walks out of the room or house. That person engages in a relaxing activity. That person reconvenes with the other as soon as possible. The Time Out may take anywhere from a few minutes to an hour or a couple of hours. However, it is not something that should last for days. That is too similar to people simply not speaking to one another after an argument. The other person needs to know that the one taking the Time Out will return when ready. The other individual is not to follow the Time Out taker around, nor approach him or her in any way, nor prematurely end the Time Out. When the Time Out is over, the issue which led to the need for the Time Out is returned to for resolution. If anger builds again, a Time Out is taken by the one feeling the anger signs. The Time Out is taken calmly. No doors are slammed. No last words are gotten in. Everything stops and one or both individuals go off to relax. If you are in a car at the time, the discussion should stop completely. The radio may be turned to soothing music or breathing techniques may be used to produce calm feelings.

It is a good idea to practice the anger management technique of taking a Time Out with a significant other. This way each party is clear on how it works and what they are to do. This makes the Time Out work more effectively in the heat of the moment.

If the Time Out procedure is held to and used consistently when needed, there may not be another destructive acting out of anger in a significant relationship again. The destructiveness of arguments and fights to the relationship, to the other partner, to the children and ultimately to oneself is avoided. In other settings and situations—like the workplace—other negative outcomes are also avoided. Perhaps one does not get a suspension, a demotion or get passed over for promotion. More importantly, one does not suffer from the tension of anger or the guilt and remorse of acting out on anger. I know that when I let my angry thoughts and feelings dissipate, I feel good about myself. Reward yourself with good feelings after managing your anger. This will reinforce the changed behavior, making it stronger and more consistent.

Time Out can be called within the first :60 Seconds of experiencing anger. The sooner it is called, the more likely the Time Out tool will be used and adhered to. So remember **C.A.R.E.**: Commit to change. Be Aware of your anger signs. Relax yourself. Exercise self-control by announcing a Time Out, either silently to yourself or vocally with your significant other. **C.A.R.E.**: *Commitment, Awareness, Relaxation, Exercise Time Outs.*

Continue on and use this book to learn more :60 Second anger management skills and to cement the changes needed to always express your normal human anger in words. Change from destructive to constructive anger expression.

:60 Second Tips: Anger Information

◆ Anger is normal.

◆ Problems occur depending on how we express anger.

◆ This book teaches the quickest way to manage your anger more effectively and constructively.

◆ Four important steps to quickly managing your anger are: Commitment, Awareness, Relaxation, Exercise Time Out or "**C.A.R.E.**"

◆ **C.A.R.E.**'s four steps will enable you to manage your anger in :60 Seconds.

CHAPTER 2

Emotion and Anger

"He who angers you conquers you."
-Elizabeth Kenny

:60 Second Information about the Four Emotions

There are four basic human emotions. They are:

- Glad
- Sad
- Scared
- Mad

It is that simple. Of course there are many variations and degrees among the four basic human emotions. Do not let that confuse you.

Many people have difficulty identifying their emotions. When asked "What do you feel about that?" or "How do you feel right now?" I invariably get back answers that are really thoughts. For example, *I feel that:*

- *My brother doesn't respect my things.*
- *My husband won't listen to me. However, if someone else makes the same suggestion, then he'll consider it.*
- *My law partner is dense.*
- *My biology teacher is terrible. All he does is read out of the textbook.*
- *My parents are so old-fashioned.*
- *I have to keep my girlfriend in line every so often.*
- *My boss is a jerk.*

None of these are feelings. They are all thoughts that one may have feelings about. In each example, the answer to "How are you feeling?" is really:

"I FEEL MAD."

The first step is to identify the feeling. The next step is to talk about what makes you feel a particular way. Remember the four basic emotions:

- Glad
- Sad
- Scared
- Mad

:60 Second Exercise: Emotions

During the course of each day, make an attempt to recognize what you are feeling.

Step 1.　Write down just the feeling.

Step 2.　Write down any cues that go along with that feeling.

Step 3.　Write down in one sentence what makes you feel the way you do.

You do not have to write down every feeling. Just pick a couple to write down each day. Also, you do not have to focus on just mad. Use instances of all four emotions. This will help you be aware of your feelings, recognize them when they happen and separate the feelings from the thoughts.

The cues for the four emotions may be:

Glad

　　a smile
　　a laugh
　　positive thoughts
　　saying something positive to someone
　　energy rather than fatigue

Sad

　　a frown
　　tears
　　drooped shoulders

head down
back slumped
thoughts of loss or loneliness
dark images
fatigue rather then energy
slowed movement

Scared

heart beating fast
cold all over
rapid and shallow breathing
tightness in the stomach
can't sit still
can't concentrate
thoughts that something bad will happen
wanting to run away

Mad

pulsing veins
clenched jaw
tensed muscles
clenched fists
hot all over
pacing
thoughts of outrage or revenge

Following is a worksheet for this exercise. Please feel free to make copies of it before filling it out.

:60 Second Emotion Worksheet

Date: _____   Time: _____

Location: _____   (home, work, school, car, store, etc.)

<u>Check off the emotion:</u>

      ☐ Glad

      ☐ Sad

      ☐ Scared

      ☐ Mad

Cues: _____

_____

_____

Thoughts:_____

_____

_____

Emotions are a part of life, of being human and alive. Just as emotions in general are normal, so too is anger normal. It is a normal human emotion. No one is ever wrong for feeling anger. There are always reasons why we get angry. The key is what we do with our anger and how we express it. There are healthy ways and there are unhealthy ways.

The first lesson in anger management is that anger is a normal emotion. Everybody feels it. In fact, there is a popular psychological test which asks the true/false question: "Sometimes I feel so angry I could throw or break something." I have often used this test to evaluate candidates for law enforcement jobs. The candidates want to create the best possible impressions, so they invariably respond "false" to this question. No one is perfect, so the results of the test can be thrown off when someone approaches it with the mind-set of creating the most positive impression. Of course, this is natural for people seeking jobs. They always want to create a good impression. It is also *natural* for people to feel so angry at times that they want to throw or break something. It simply refers to the idea that might come to mind, but must not be acted upon. Remember, it is normal to think these things, but there is a big difference between thinking something and acting on it.

:60 Second Goal

Your ultimate goal will be to express anger in words using a non-threatening tone. You will learn how to do this and eventually become able to say:

"I feel angry. I feel that way because...."

:60 Second Tips: The Four Basic Emotions

♦ There are four basic human emotions. They are Glad, Sad, Scared and Mad.

♦ When asked how they feel, people commonly express their thoughts instead of their feelings.

♦ Use the :60 Second Emotion Worksheet to keep track of your feelings and the cues and thoughts associated with them.

♦ All emotions, including anger, are normal.

♦ There are always reasons why we get angry.

♦ There are healthy ways to deal with and express our anger.

♦ We may think about hostile acts, but not act on them.

CHAPTER 3

When Anger Leads to Problems

*"He who establishes his argument by noise and
command shows that his reason is weak."*
-Michel de Montaigne

As is true of all our emotions, whether glad, sad, scared or mad, anger probably had some survival value for our species. The adrenaline rush, the tunneling of vision, the rapidity of heartbeat and the flow of blood to the extremities probably made us better fighters or hunters. However, in modern society this "fight or flight" response to anger is no longer viable. Actions taken in anger may be viewed as out of control rage, frenzied behavior or even illegal acts. Angry acts are certainly destructive to relationships, to others and ultimately to the self. If not expressed, however, anger can lead to the development of ulcers, headaches, back and neck pain, anxiety, panic attacks and depression. The serious downsides to both bottling up anger and giving in to angry acts should be motivation enough for most people to change and learn new, more effective ways of handling and expressing anger.

:60 Second Distinction
Remember that there is an important distinction between expressing anger in words and acting out in anger. The former is a positive response; the latter is a negative response.

Calmly stating "I feel angry right now, because…" is an example of expressing anger in words and is the healthiest, most constructive way to express angry feelings. You will be much more likely to be heard and responded to in a positive way. You will get results. Your new method of anger expression will become self-reinforcing. It works and you will be rewarded and therefore encouraged to use this method again in the future. Momentum will build, making it easier and easier to say: **"I feel angry now, because…"**

The use of cursing, shouting, name-calling and put-downs, while only verbal, are not constructive and are really negative methods of act-ing on one's anger. These modes of expression are hurtful to others and can be as or even more hurtful than physical aggression. In many cases, emotional scars last much longer than physical ones. Clearly, physical acts of any type, including slamming doors, throwing or breaking objects, pushing, grabbing, slapping, hitting or even using a weapon, are all exam-ples of acting out in anger. They are also part of the legal definition of physical abuse. It does not matter whether you grab someone by the arm or you punch him in the face. The law considers both to be physical abuse and you can be put in jail.

There has been a tendency in our society to zero in on men as phys-ical or emotional abusers. However, our focus in this book is on healthy versus unhealthy, constructive versus destructive ways of expressing anger. Women are equally as likely as men to express their anger in destructive ways. Research has shown that often women are more effec-tive verbally than men, thus they tend to have the upper hand in the ver-bal part of arguments. Some men may turn to physical actions to regain control. In this book you will notice that there will be an equal number of case histories involving males and females.

At their core, most arguments have to do with control and power. When we become angry and argue, we frequently are trying to retain or gain dominance in a forceful way, whether by words or actions. The focus of this book and the cases discussed will be anger expression in general and not just on physically violent anger expression.

In my workshops and one-on-one counseling sessions, I have noticed that there is not one global prototype for individuals with anger problems. Traditionally, anger management treatment has been conducted using a shotgun approach. All individuals are given all techniques at once. My research has shown that there are different types of loss of anger control. This suggests that treatment should be tailored to the individual types of anger problems. Help needs to be specific for the three different types of anger problems. In this regard, we will focus on anger internalization, over-controlled anger and under-controlled anger.

Anger internalization is the act of keeping emotions bottled up. People who suppress their anger are referred to as *anger internalizers*. They may have strong internal prohibitions against expressing anger. As a result, they behave passively. They do not release their anger in any way and often become sick from it. This is what is meant when therapists say that the anger is turned against the self. Anger internalizers may suffer from ulcers, headaches, pain, depression, anxiety and panic attacks. They sometimes try to express their anger in the things they do *not* do or say, perhaps withholding what others ask of them in order to get back at those with whom they are angry.

In an article for the professional journal *Violence and Victims*, another therapist and I wrote about the fact that **over-controlled anger** occurs when an individual possesses strong controls against the expression of anger (Hershorn and Rosenbaum, *Violence and Victims*, 1991). Anger builds and builds until some event, major or minor, triggers an intense, explosive outburst. The duration of the outburst is short and the person usually feels guilty and remorseful afterwards. The objects of the anger are invariably limited to "safe" ones, such as inanimate objects or an individual's significant other.

Under-controlled anger, we explained in the journal article, occurs when an individual has few internal controls against the expression of anger. Outbursts of anger are more frequent but less intense than in the over-controlled person and can be directed at any number of objects including friends, bosses, teachers, strangers, significant others and even police. Generally, adults tend be over-controlled in their anger while adolescents tend to be under-controlled in their anger. Both adults and teens can be anger internalizers. These distinctions, of course, are not absolute. There is blending of the three types of anger expression across age populations and even within individuals.

Research has shown that adults and adolescents have been under the influence of some substance (alcohol or drugs) in about 50 percent of the cases in which anger has been expressed destructively or violently. If you find that you have a substance abuse or dependency problem, you will need to address it through the various available treatment programs. However, with regard to anger problems, you may not need to have an actual substance abuse or dependency problem. Simply using alcohol or a drug on a limited or "social" basis may be detrimental to your ability to manage your angry feelings. It is not a good idea to try to seriously communicate with others at a time when you or they have been using alcohol or drugs.

Here are three psychological, paper-and-pencil inventories which serve as self-tests for problematic anger expression. These will provide you with a baseline against which to measure progress as you continue reading, practicing and utilizing :60 Second anger management tools. Let's establish some baselines, so we can measure our progress later.

:60 Second Test #1: Anger Problem

At some point, everyone experiences anger. But how can you know when your anger is becoming a problem, perhaps even a handicap, in your life? Here are a few signs that will tell you when your anger is creating problems for you.

1. *When it is too frequent.* There are many situations in which feeling angry is justified and proper. However, we often get angry when it is not necessary or useful. You must begin to make a distinction between the times when it is all right to be angry and when getting angry isn't warranted.

2. *When it is too intense.* Anger is something that occurs at different levels of intensity. A small or moderate amount of anger can often work to your advantage. But high degrees of anger seldom produce positive results.

3. *When it lasts too long.* When anger is prolonged, you maintain a level of arousal or stress that goes beyond normal limits. We often think of this as "making too much of something." When anger does not subside, your body's systems are prevented from returning to normal levels,

making you susceptible to further aggravation and annoyance. Thus, it becomes easier to get angry the next time something goes wrong. Furthermore, when anger lasts too long, resolution of conflict becomes more difficult and eventually impossible.

4. ***When it leads to aggression.*** When you feel you have been abused or treated unfairly, you may want to lash out at the person who has offended you. Anger, particularly when intense and personal, pushes for an aggressive response. Your muscles get tense, your voice gets louder and you clench your fists and stare sharply. There is then a greater tendency to act on impulse. Aggressive acts are sure to get you into trouble. Verbal aggression, such as calling someone a jerk, and physical aggression, such as slapping the offender, are ineffective ways of dealing with conflict. If your anger makes you aggressive, you have a problem.

5. ***When it disturbs school, work or relationships.*** When your anger interferes with doing a good job or makes it hard for people to relate to you, then it becomes costly. It prevents concentration on your work and keeps you from being satisfied with what you do. Anger may cost you salary raises or promotions at work, as well as repel people and make it difficult for them to like you.

Uncontrolled anger is always ugly, but managed anger does not have to be negative. Learning to use its positive qualities will make your life a lot more productive. Check in with yourself by answering these five questions about your anger:

1. Is it too frequent? _____ Yes _____ No

2. Is it too intense? _____ Yes _____ No

3. Does it last too long? _____ Yes _____ No

4. Does it lead to aggression? _____ Yes _____ No

5. Does it disturb school, work or relationships? _____ Yes _____ No

If the answers for some or all of the questions are yes, there is a problem. When you start being able to answer no, you are making progress. We will return to this :60 Second test later.

:60 Second Test #2: Anger Description

Part I.

Following are a number of statements that people use to describe themselves. Read each statement and then write the number (1, 2, 3 or 4) which indicates how you *generally* feel on the line provided. Remember that there are no right or wrong answers. Do not spend too much time on any one statement, but give the answer which seems to *best* describe how you *generally* feel. Fill in the line with 1, 2, 3 or 4 based on the following measures:

1 = *Almost never* 3 = *Often*
2 = *Sometimes* 4 = *Almost always*

How I Generally Feel

_____ I am quick tempered.

_____ I have a fiery temper.

_____ I am a hotheaded person.

_____ I get angry when I'm slowed down by others' mistakes.

_____ I feel annoyed when I am not given recognition for doing good work.

_____ I fly off the handle.

_____ When I get mad, I say nasty things.

_____ It makes me furious when I am criticized in front of others.

_____ When I get frustrated, I feel like hitting someone.

_____ I feel infuriated when I do a good job and get a poor evaluation.

Part II.

Everyone feels angry or even furious from time to time, but people differ in the ways that they react when they are angry. The following list includes statements that people use to describe their reactions when they feel *angry* or *furious*. Read each statement and then fill in the line with the number (1, 2, 3 or 4) which indicates how *often* you *generally* react or behave in the manner described when you are feeling angry or furious. Remember that there are no right or wrong answers. Do not spend too much time on any one statement.

1 = *Almost never*   3 = *Often*
2 = *Sometimes*   4 = *Almost always*

When Angry or Furious . . .

_____ I control my temper.

_____ I express my anger.

_____ I keep things in.

_____ I am patient with others.

_____ I pout or sulk.

_____ I withdraw from people.

_____ I make sarcastic remarks to others.

_____ I keep my cool.

_____ I do things like slam doors.

_____ I boil inside, but I don't show it.

_____ I control my behavior.

_____ I argue with others.

_____ I tend to harbor grudges that I don't tell anyone about.

_____ I strike out at whatever infuriates me.

_____ I can stop myself from losing my temper.

_____ I am secretly quite critical of others.

_____ I am angrier than I am willing to admit.

_____ I calm down faster than most other people.

_____ I say nasty things.

_____ I try to be tolerant and understanding.

_____ I'm irritated a great deal more than people are aware of.

_____ I lose my temper.

_____ If someone annoys me, I'm apt to tell him or her how I feel.

_____ I control my angry feelings.

Now, calculate your scores for Part I and Part II separately.

Part I   _____

Part II   _____

Compare your numbers to the scores given in Table A below. If your totals are equal to or greater than the numbers in the table, you may have an anger problem.

TABLE A

	Part I	Part II
Male Adults	21	23
Female Adults	22	17

Part I measures a general tendency to experience and express anger without specific provocation. Individuals with scores of twenty-one or higher frequently experience angry feelings and often feel that they are treated unfairly by others. They are likely to experience a great deal of frustration. They may express, suppress or control their anger.

Part II is a general index of the frequency that anger is expressed, regardless of the direction of expression (inward, outward or overly controlled). If your score is comparable to or higher than indicated in Table A, you may experience intense angry feelings, which may be suppressed, expressed in aggressive behavior or both. You may manifest anger in many facets of behavior. You may have difficulty in relationships and are at risk to develop medical and psychological disorders. There is a chance that you may develop high blood pressure. If your scores are much higher than those in the table, there is even a risk for vulnerability to coronary artery disease and heart attacks. The need to change is obvious. Learning :60 Second anger management skills may be the best thing you have ever done for yourself. We will return to these tests later to check on your progress.

Having taken the tests, you now may realize you have a problem. It is important for you to understand that you are not bad or sick or crazy because you have an anger problem. It is the behavior that is unacceptable and destructive.

Anger management problems are learned and can be unlearned. For example, 50 percent of all physically abusive individuals either witnessed or experienced physical abuse as they were growing up. Through modeling, a powerful learning mechanism, they learned to use such methods themselves. To these individuals, abuse, or the acting out of anger verbally or physically, became an acceptable method of expressing anger and dealing with others. Some people who grew up in households with parents who made them angry but stifled their expressions of anger by being punitive or abusive may have become over-controlled in their experiences and expressions of anger. Others who grew up in broken and chaotic families where there were few rules and limits but much acting out of anger may have become under-controlled in their experiences and expressions of anger. Let me assure you there are many reasons why individuals come to have problems with anger. They are not simply "bad" people.

:60 Second Case Study: "Big Brother"

Dennis came to me when he was forty years old. He was a professional working in his own successful practice, married for twelve years with three young sons and living in a comfortable home in a pleasant suburb. He had been verbally and physically abusing his wife throughout their marriage. His wife had finally told her parents, his parents and Dennis that she wanted a separation and why.

When he came to me, Dennis was desperate for help. We focused our work on identifying and changing his behavior and the thinking that led to that behavior. Dennis, it turned out, did not grow up in a violent home. He did not witness abuse. He did not experience abuse. He never remembered his parents as big arguers. They mostly kept to themselves, away from each other.

In the course of our work, after his anger was under control and being expressed appropriately, Dennis wondered why he had abused his wife. Over time, he came to realize that the key was his birth order. Dennis is the oldest of three boys. He had grown up physically dominating his younger brothers. When he wanted something and they refused, Dennis used his age, size and strength to get what he wanted. It worked. His aggression was as simple as that. No deep, dark, hidden secret or issue. Dennis carried this behavior into his marriage, using his size and strength to get what he wanted, to maintain control and to dominate his wife. Using physical force had always worked for him. His problematic anger expression was reinforced because it worked. He used force and aggression because it was effective.

Dennis came for help feeling terrible about himself, but he learned he was not bad. He had simply learned and retained bad behaviors. The good news is that he unlearned them and took on a whole new repertoire of effective communication and negotiation skills. After I worked with him individually and the abuse was eliminated, Dennis' wife joined the counseling sessions to strengthen their relationship skills. As it turned out, Dennis' wife was just as he described, "much better at expressing what she wants to say than me. I would get frustrated and resort to the only thing left in my arsenal. Being physical."

The purpose of this case history is to point out that it was not Dennis, but his behavior that was the problem. This is a real-life example of what you have read so far. Although Dennis judged himself and felt guilt and shame, I did not judge him. We came to see that his problematic anger expression had some instrumental purpose. It was learned throughout his youth and reinforced because it worked. He carried this into adulthood and ultimately risked losing his wife and family. However, by seeking help, he not only did not lose, he gained.

:60 Second Tips: Anger Acts

♦ Remember, angry acts take a toll on relationships, others and the self.

♦ Know that angry acts may be illegal.

♦ Accept that there is a need to change.

♦ Distinguish expressing anger in words from acting out on anger.

♦ Say, "I feel angry right now, because..."

♦ Recall that men and women are equally likely to express anger in destructive ways.

♦ Anger has to do with exerting power and control.

♦ There is anger internalization, over-controlled anger and under-controlled anger.

♦ There are tools for each type of problem.

♦ Alcohol and drugs play a large role in anger problems.

♦ You are not bad, sick or crazy.

♦ There are reasons for your anger management problem.

♦ You have learned problematic behaviors and you can unlearn them.

CHAPTER 4

The Anger Management Model

"Discretion is being able to raise your eyebrow instead of your voice."

-Anon

O ver the years I have conducted many anger management workshops. These are short-term, initial interventions of six ninety-minute group sessions. Most people do not come voluntarily or willingly. They are either court-ordered, pushed in by partners who are about to or have already left, told by employers who give the option of workshop or termination or by schools which give the option of workshop or ten days suspension. These anger management workshops have been my most rewarding experiences as a clinician. I have seen remarkable turnarounds in relatively little time. You, too, can make a remarkable turnaround.

In the workshops most people come in expecting to be judged and not understood or accepted. They are very defensive. The first session is spent listening to how each participant came to be at the workshop, hearing their individual stories. They speak of just snapping or of being provoked. Common themes of loss of control and lack of responsibility are expressed. I listen and empathize. I do not confront. I work to build acceptance and trust. Then together we begin the important lessons on managing problematic anger expression.

:60 Second Exercise: Anger Management

Just as the workshop participants told their stories of how they came to be at the meetings, on the following lines write down how you came to be using this book. You can start with "My therapist told me to do it" or "My significant other bought it for me as a last-ditch effort before leaving me." Don't stop there, though. Go on to explain what led up to you picking up the book or someone asking you to read and use it:

_____

_____

_____

_____

_____

_____

_____

_____

_____

_____

If you are like almost everyone I've worked with, you probably wrote stories of being angered and provoked, of having your buttons pushed and then just snapping. You are not alone. Everyone feels that at times in their lives they have been provoked to the boiling point and suddenly lost control of their tempers. You probably are incited to anger by situations, events or other people. Nobody gets angry for no reason. You feel you lose your temper and self-control because of the heat of the emotions you experience. You do not perceive the subtle buildup of feelings, sensations and behaviors which feed each other. Because of these strong emotions and your focus on what the other person is saying or doing, you have little opportunity to notice what is going on inside of you.

Thoughts are simply things we say to ourselves. They are just statements we make in our head without verbally expressing them. This is
why thoughts can also be considered self-statements. Workshop attendees had many negative self-statements about attending the workshops
and about themselves because of their anger management problems.
Negative self-statements can be disputed and replaced with counteract-
ing positive self-statements. We can control what we choose to think
about the world, other people and ourselves. For example, workshop
members often expressed the thought that they resented having to be the
one to come to the meetings. This negative thought could be replaced
with the positive thought, *Since I have to be here, I might as well get something
out of it.* Workshop attendees often harbored feelings of guilt and shame.
They thought they were bad, sick or crazy. How else could they explain
having to see a "shrink." The fact is that, as a clinical psychologist, I work
with normal, everyday people who are simply having problems in their
lives. They are functioning and contributing members of society with
positive as well as negative traits.

All of us have positive and negative aspects to our personalities.
Those individuals who seek treatment are usually demoralized about or
overwhelmed by their problems and are tired of living with them. Those
who are pushed by others to seek treatment are also overwhelmed and
probably demoralized by their problems, but haven't had the motivation
to seek help on their own. Therapy or counseling is a process of "remor-
alization." Individuals take on the more objective viewpoint of the therapist and begin to use the tools offered to change their problem-causing
thoughts and actions. Workshop participants are encouraged to dispute
or replace negative self-statements with positive ones such as:

·   *I am not bad, sick or crazy.*
·   *I learned faulty behaviors and ways of thinking and I can unlearn them.*
·   *There are reasons why I have acted as I have.*
·   *I can change.*

:60 Second Exercise: Negative and Positive Self-statements

Just as I ask workshop members to do, I would like you to write
down negative self-statements you have about reading this book and
about yourself for having anger problems. Then in the column to the

right, write down a positive self-statement to dispute or replace the negative one. Notice how you can *choose* to think differently about things and about yourself. I have given an example to help you get started.

Negative Self-statement	**Positive Self-statement**
Example: I'm ticked off at my wife for making me read this dumb book.	I'm reading this book to save my marriage—and it might help me in other areas of my life, too.

1) _____   1) _____

2) _____   2) _____

3) _____   3) _____

4) _____   4) _____

5) _____   5) _____

The first lesson of my workshops has to do with dispelling clients' notions that *I just snap, I just go off* or *I don't know what comes over me.* All these rationalizations imply lack of control. If there truly is no control, then there can be no help. Many attendees at workshops come in with these accounts. After we listen, accept and empathize to establish trust and safety, we dispute the notions by throwing out questions such as:

- *Did you hit him as hard as you possibly could?*
- *Did you break your most valuable piece of china?*
- *Did you go off on your boss or some co-worker who was in the wrong place at the wrong time?*
- *Did you choose to punch him, scratch him or slap him?*
- *Did you knock over your computer monitor or throw your stapler across the room?*

Hearing these questions, individuals invariably realize that they indeed were making choices about their anger expression and exercising some level of self-control. One can literally see the "aha" that comes over their facial expressions. They learn that anger *is* something over which they have control. They feel comfortable acknowledging this, because the fear of judgment has been lessened within the workshop environment. The purpose of therapeutic workshops and counseling is to understand and change behaviors, not condemn those who exhibit them.

The next lesson has to do with provocation. I often hear statements like:

- *She made me do it.*
- *He knows just how to push my buttons.*
- *He dissed me in front of my friends.*
- *She got right in my face.*
- *She grabbed the baby, the car keys and blocked the doorway.*
- *He called me out.*
- *He called my girlfriend a tramp.*

A client is often quite relieved to hear that I agree that another person or a situation provoked understandable anger. However, I always remind him that although he may have been legitimately provoked to anger, it was his *choice* to express that anger in a destructive way or to negatively act out. It does not matter what the provoking person said or did or what seems fair or not. Ultimately, an individual has no control over what other people do; she only has control over herself and her own actions. Once we establish that an individual's anger is hurtful to others or himself and that such angry acting out is unacceptable, the client becomes ready to accept responsibility for his actions and wants to change. In the workshops, he or she begins to raise a clamor for help and guidance. "Okay, Doc, so now what can I do about it?"

Once people realize they do have control, the are empowered to change. They are no longer helplessly caught up in a destructive, hurtful cycle of anger feeding more anger. The fact that I am readily able to offer a number of specific anger management techniques and tools supports their realization that control is possible and they can make choices. It becomes okay to accept these lessons, because they are being offered concrete, immediate methods to create change.

Following is a series of chapters dealing with the specific tools for change. There will be more short tests to determine problematic drinking and drug use. There will be case examples to encourage the transfer of what you have learned to the real world. There will be homework and exercises to perform that will take you out of the passive mode and move you to action. There will be discussions of how, when and where to seek professional help, as well as examples of self-help support groups. You will note and rate your own changes and improvements and will learn to acknowledge and reward yourself for your efforts. You will be instructed to ask for feedback from others, such as spouses, teachers, friends, colleagues, girlfriends, boyfriends, bosses and fellow employees. Feelings of self-worth and self-esteem will blossom and grow as your secret anger is brought out in the light to be understood and overcome.

:60 Second Tips: Working Through Anger

♦ Be aware that you are provoked to feel anger. Nobody gets angry for no reason.

♦ Tap into what is going on inside of you rather than focusing on what others say or do.

♦ Know we can control what we choose to think about the world, others and ourselves.

♦ Replace negative self-statements with positive ones.

♦ Remember you do not just snap. You are in control when you act on anger.

♦ Even if legitimately provoked, it is only you who chooses to act out on anger.

♦ Learn that acting out on your anger is destructive and ultimately hurts you.

♦ Accept that you have control only over yourself. You have no control over what other people say or do.

♦ Accept responsibility for your actions and acknowledge your power of choice and self-control.

♦ Be empowered to accept change.

♦ Acquire knowledge about many concrete, immediate ways to change.

CHAPTER 5

Anger is Okay

"You are never given a wish without also being given the power to make it come true. You may have to work for it, however."

-Richard Bach

Remember that it is okay to feel anger; it is just how we choose to express it that may cause problems. Faulty notions about anger have already been dispelled in the previous chapters. I hope you now realize that you are in control when you express anger destructively. Let's practice.

:60 Second Exercise: Angry Acts

Write down examples of your own angry acts. Then, next to each one, write the most extreme version of the act that you can think of. I have given some examples to help you get started.

My Angry Act	The Most Extreme Version
Example #1: I threw the plate at the wall.	I threw the plate into his face, which required many stitches at the hospital.
Example #2: I cursed at her.	I cursed her out, made her cry and then I said I wished I had never met her.

1) _____   1) _____

_____   _____

_____   _____

2) _____   2) _____

_____   _____

_____   _____

3) _____   3) _____

_____   _____

_____   _____

4) _____   4) _____

_____   _____

_____   _____

Are there differences between what you actually did and the extreme version of what you could have done? Do you think you made choices and possessed some level of control in these instances?

:60 Second Exercise: Anger Provocation

In this exercise you will see that while you may have been provoked to feel anger, it was up to you to choose how to express your anger—in an ineffective and/or destructive way or in a positive, constructive way. Common self-statements about provocation will be listed. As you will see, these statements imply a lack of self-control in the reaction to the person provoking anger. You are to dispute the provocation self-statements in the column on the right. Be sure your disputing self-statements indicate the angry person's reaction was his or her *choice*.

Self-statements of Provocation

1) She made me so angry, I hit her.

2) He insulted me in front of my friends. I had to slap him.

3) He told me dinner was terrible, so I dumped his plate of food in his lap.

Disputing Self-statements

1) _____

_____

_____

2) _____

_____

_____

3) _____

_____

_____

If you are having difficulty with this exercise, here are examples of self-statements that dispute the provoking statements given:

1) She made me angry, so I *chose* to hit her.
2) He insulted and embarrassed me in public, so I *chose* to slap him in front of the others.
3) His criticism angered and hurt me, so I *chose* to dump the plate in his lap.

Now write down some self-statements of provocation you have experienced. In the column on the right, dispute those statements.

1) _____

_____

_____

2) _____

_____

_____

1) _____

_____

_____

2) _____

_____

_____

3) _____   3) _____

_____   _____

_____   _____

4) _____   4) _____

_____   _____

_____   _____

Realizing that you are in control and responsible for your behavior will empower you to feel in charge and not helpless in the face of your problem. :60 Second anger management techniques will help you strengthen and expand your control. They worked for Jerry and they will work for you.

:60 Second Case Study: "The Mountain Man"

Jerry was in his early twenties. He was a big, burly truck driver with a full beard. Jerry had a girlfriend, but he also liked to drink in bars. Jerry got into fights with everybody. Eventually he was locked up for fighting. This led him to be court ordered to an anger management workshop. My first impression of him was that he would be a tough case; he was court ordered against his will and used to having his way because of his size. The group felt intimidated by him. In reality, he was more intimidated by us. Jerry turned out to be one of those gentle giants. He opened up slowly and revealed himself to be intelligent and articulate. He did well and made good contributions and graduated from the program. He stopped his violence.

About one year later, I found myself working late at about 7:00 P.M. The phone rang and purely by chance I answered it. It was Jerry. He was calling from another state where he had moved with his girlfriend. He reported that there had been no more arrests nor bar fights nor abuse of his girlfriend. He had stopped drinking and lost weight. They were engaged and planning to marry. Jerry thanked me. He said he had been brought up to believe that a man does not express his feelings. The first time he had ever opened up about himself was in our group workshop.

He learned that it was okay to have emotions and to share them with others. Jerry learned that he was okay, he could control his anger and he could be accepted by others. He could accept himself. The six-week program not only changed his way of dealing with anger, it changed his life and he just wanted me to know. I was deeply moved by this call. After twenty-one years in practice, a spontaneous moment of appreciation such as this still stands out and remembering it makes me feel contentment about helping a person to change. The opportunity afforded by this book to reach a large population is a great and gratifying one.

I hope Jerry's case gives you great promise, hope and positive feelings and that you will be eager to continue your own journey. We will be in the process of change together. I will be cheering you on and will be in your corner. I hope, as with most anger management workshop participants, you will go from feeling an obligation to read the book to really desiring to use the book and its tools. As with therapy patients who approach the process with trepidation, I hope you will realize that there is an adventure to be had with a faithful ally alongside to guide and urge you on. Like many workshop attendees, I hope you are thinking *Okay, Doc, so now what do we do about it?* The fact that there are ready answers will cement what was learned so far. When I show you how to change, you will find it becomes even easier to accept responsibility and do it.

Continue reading. The best is yet to come.

:60 Second Tips: Anger Management

- ◆ Remember, it is okay to feel anger; it is just how we choose to express it that may cause problems.
- ◆ Realize that even when you are provoked to anger, you can dispute the notion that you have no control or are not responsible for your angry responses by changing your self-statements.
- ◆ Know that you are not helpless; you are in charge.
- ◆ See the process of change as an adventure.
- ◆ Remember that I am your ally in this process.

PART II

MANAGING YOUR ANGER

"If you are patient in one moment of anger, you will escape a hundred days of sorrow."
-Chinese Proverb

CHAPTER 6

Making the Commitment

"Something must happen—that explains most human commitments."

-Albert Camus

Let's return for a moment to the case of "Big Brother." When Dennis came to me on the very first day of treatment, he told me that he had vowed to himself never to abuse his wife either verbally or physically again. Many individuals make this promise to themselves and to those people affected by their anger. However, they make this promise as a form of denial of the problem and the need for help. They never learn to change the behavior or replace destructive habits with constructive ones. Frequently, the promise is made and broken over and over again. Destroying trust like this becomes a dangerous cycle that can harm or kill relationships.

In Dennis' case, although he said he had made this promise only one time, he had never before wanted to change. He had wanted his wife to remain intimidated. He had made her feel responsible for and worthy of his abuse. He had worn down her self-esteem and she accepted his treatment of her for twelve years. Her acceptance was not out of some deep-rooted need to be treated badly. Dennis' wife felt shame and so she bought into the concept that she was a bad wife and mother. She had learned to think this way. The shame also kept her from telling anyone. Eventually, the women's movement, along with information and education on spousal abuse, gave her the courage to stand up for herself.

Dennis became committed to keeping his vow. After our sessions, he never verbally or physically attacked his wife again. At the initial workshop meeting, he also took one of our important first steps. Upon entry to a workshop or individual counseling, I ask everyone to make a commitment to me and, more importantly, to themselves to never act destructively on their anger again. I am asking you now to do the same.

:60 Second Exercise: Commitment

Write down a commitment about changing below.

_____

_____

_____

_____

_____

_____

_____

_____

Post your written commitment on your bathroom mirror or your refrigerator or your computer. Post a mental version in your mind. Visualize it in your mind's eye, because this picture is worth a thousand words. This is not the whole process of changing, but it is an important step. Make a commitment to yourself. When you do this, you have taken a most important second step. The first one was picking up this book!

Another important point to remember is that the focus on changing must be on yourself. Ultimately, you can never control anyone or anything other than yourself. As you change, however, things and people around you will change. Sometimes for the better, perhaps sometimes not. There is one strange phenomenon in the treatment of spouse abusers, for example. When the abuser stops abusing, the victim sometimes becomes abusive. This is the result of pent up anger and resentment and the reduction of fear. If this begins happening to you, it is not your cue to go backwards. The other person needs to work on his or her anger and expression of it. Buy another copy of this book and offer it to the person. Otherwise stay away from trying to change this individual. Stay focused on changing yourself. If a relationship ends, you will need your new abilities to establish another one. If you feel your significant other has an anger problem, don't get caught up in thinking about how unfair it is that you are working on your anger alone. He or she may infuriate you, but it is you who has chosen to act on anger. Work on yourself. Worry about the other person later. Sometimes when a couple enters marital counseling, for example, the destructive expression of anger can actually escalate and become dangerous. The first step is to get the problematic anger expression under control. Later, the issues which lead to anger in a relationship, such as finances, childrearing, religious and cultural differences or how to spend leisure time, can be dealt with. The same holds true for anger during a separation and divorce. The anger must be dealt with first, then the issues and disagreements can be worked upon.

:60 Second Tips: Problematic Anger

◆ Recognize that false promises to change come from denying the problem and not getting help for it.

◆ Accept that false promises destroy trust in relationships.

◆ Realize it is crucial to make a commitment never to act out on anger again.

◆ Write down your commitment and post it in a spot that you will see often.

◆ Remember, you only have control over yourself, therefore, it is up to you to change.

◆ Realize couples counseling can be dangerous if individual anger has not been brought under control.

CHAPTER 7

Early Warning Signs, Cues and Triggers

"This one step–choosing a goal and sticking to it–changes everything."
-Scott Reed

Whether you are an anger internalizer or an "anger-actor-outer," the following equally applies. Everyone experiences signs that he or she is getting angry. No one just "explodes." No one just "implodes." You learned some fundamentals in chapter 1 and we will now go into great depth and detail in teaching you how to manage your anger in a positive fashion. This takes some learning and work, so read on.

Identify your anger. Remember, there are three types of cues that accompany the emotion of anger. They are Physiological (physical sensations), Behavioral (actions) and Cognitive (thoughts).

Physiological cues might include:
· Feeling your face flush
· Blood rushing through your veins
· Your heart pounding
· Your breathing becoming faster, shallower or unsteady
· Feeling hot or feeling cold
· Feeling a pain in your neck (hence the expression "pain in the neck")

Behavioral cues might include:
· Clenching your fists
· Clenching your jaw
· Grinding your teeth

·   Tensing and flexing your muscles
·   Pacing around the room
·   An inability to sit or stand still

Cognitive cues might include such thoughts as:

·   *He did this to me out of spite.*
·   *She did this to me purposely.*
·   *I can't believe he did that.*
·   *No one talks to me like that.*
·   *I'll show him.*
·   *This is unacceptable.*

Thoughts are like unspoken words we say to ourselves and hear in our minds. The more we think about what is angering us, the angrier we get. It is a vicious cycle. The anger fuels the thoughts. The thoughts fuel the anger. We will return to this in more detail later.

:60 Second Exercise: Anger Cues

List your own personal physiological, behavioral and cognitive cues of anger.

Physiological

_____

_____

_____

_____

Behavioral

_____

_____

_____

_____

Cognitive

_____

_____

_____

_____

These cues are your early warning signs. The sooner you can recognize them, the better chance you have to change what you do with your anger. You are less caught up in the wave of anger and more able to act differently than in the past.

Everybody has common triggers for anger. Remember that your anger may be provoked, but you are responsible for how you deal with it. You may keep the anger in and let it build up. You may act out on it immediately or express it appropriately. Triggers may include your partner coming home late without calling; your boss dumping an urgent assignment on your desk five minutes before the end of the workday; someone criticizing you; your children leaving their toys laying around; getting a traffic ticket; a neighbor repeatedly playing loud music; or your students not paying attention while you are trying to teach.

An English teacher at a school I attended once threatened to jump out of the window from our third floor classroom for just such an incident; he had grown angry after repeatedly asking students to stop talking and pay attention to his lesson. He actually stood on top of a three-foot bookshelf, swung the window wide open and yelled, "I'm going to jump, I'm going to jump." The tension was thankfully broken when one of my classmates hollered back, "Jump!" Everyone—including the teacher—started laughing. The joke helped the teacher realize just how extreme and absurd his response to his angry feelings was. He probably never intended to jump, but this story shows just how far anger can push some people to react. It also shows how important it is for us all to recognize the triggers that make us angry, so we can head off anger before it gets the better of us.

:60 Second Exercise: Anger Triggers

List your common triggers:

1) _____

_____

_____

2) _____

_____

_____

3) _____

_____

_____

4) _____

_____

_____

5) _____

_____

_____

By becoming aware of your most common triggers, you will be fore-warned to start monitoring cues or signs of anger. You will be able to say to yourself, "Okay, this situation is familiar. It has triggered my anger before. I know I need to deal with it differently." How to deal with it will come shortly. But for now, you are learning to be your own good counselor, teacher and therapist.

:60 Second Exercise: Anger Rating

In this exercise you will keep a journal to track your anger. By keeping a journal you will be altering your patterns and dealing with anger in new ways. Journaling itself is known to mental health workers to be an excellent way of recognizing and then changing many behaviors. In the journal you will be expressing your anger rather than keeping it in (suppressing) or inappropriately acting on it. If this cannot be done in the heat of the moment because you are too emotional and not objective enough to be rational, remove yourself from the situation and journal it as soon as possible. This will help you learn a great deal about your anger. Look for repeating patterns. What are you common triggers? What are your common behaviors? What are the common consequences? With this information you will be more prepared to intervene early and change old patterns.

Use the Anger Journal that follows to rate your anger on a scale of 1 to 10, 1 being the least angry, 10 being the most:

1 - 2 - 3:   Irritated, Frustrated, Annoyed
4 - 5 - 6:   Angry, Mad, Irate
7 - 8 - 9:   Enraged, Furious, Explosive
     10:    Physically and/or Verbally Abusive

On the next two pages, you will find the journal format you should use for recording this information. Make copies of the blank pages before filling in any information. The next time you experience great anger over something, use the journal to record information about the incident. Write down the date and time, what led up to your anger, what you did with it and what happened after.

Anger Journal

Date:

Intensity: 1 – 2 – 3   4 – 5 – 6   7 – 8 – 9   10
                  (Irritated)   (Mad)   (Furious)   (Abusive)

Physiological
Signs

_____

_____

_____

_____

Behavioral
Signs

_____

_____

_____

_____

Cognitive
Signs

_____

_____

_____

_____

Trigger(s)

_____

_____

_____

What You
Did With it

_____

_____

_____

What Happened
Afterward

_____

_____

_____

Were You Under
the Influence of
Alcohol or Drugs?   Yes _____   No _____

:60 Second Tips: Anger Cues and Triggers

♦ Remember, no one just explodes or implodes.

♦ Identify your own personal anger signals, signs or cues.

♦ Know that cues can be physiological (physical sensations), behavioral (actions) and cognitive (thoughts).

♦ Recognize that there is a vicious, escalating cycle of angry thoughts fueling angry feelings, which in turn fuel more angry thoughts and so on.

♦ Realize cues are your early warning signs that you are feeling angry.

♦ Accept that the earlier you recognize you are angry, the better your chances are to change what you do with your anger.

♦ Appreciate that everyone has his or her own typical and repetitive triggers for anger.

♦ Become aware of the common triggers that forewarn your anger, so you can start monitoring your cues.

♦ Learn to say, "Okay, this situation is familiar. It has triggered anger before. I know I need to deal with it differently."

♦ Copy and use the anger journal format to learn about your anger.

♦ Use a journal as a constructive method of expressing your anger.

CHAPTER 8

Time Out Isn't Just for Children

"Nothing is so strong as gentleness and nothing is so gentle as real strength."
-Ralph W. Sockman

Time Out is not a disciplinary technique solely for handling children. It is an effective anger management tool for adults and is being introduced here as a :60 Second emergency, stopgap procedure. When you become aware of any signs of anger, you need to take a Time Out from the situation. It is *your* responsibility to call a Time Out—no one else's. Stay away from the situation or the person who provoked your anger for as long as it takes you to cool down. During the Time Out, engage in something antithetical to anger: **relaxation**.

There are many activities that are relaxing. These can include: walking, running, listening to music, calling a friend, taking a bath, practicing meditation, roller-blading, biking, going to a local bookstore or shopping at the mall.

:60 Second Exercise: Relaxing
List all of the activities you now engage in that you find relaxing.

1) _____

2) _____

3) _____

4) _____

5) _____

Be ready to use any of these activities during a Time Out. Plan ahead as to what you will do to relax during a Time Out.

Do not engage in anything aggressive like hitting a punching bag or driving fast. This maintains the association of feeling angry and acting it out. Do not use alcohol or drugs during the Time Out. When you have cooled down, return to the situation or person that led to your angry feelings and touch base. This way the other person will not object to the Time Out, which could be corrupted into a form of "blowing off" or ignoring another person. If you feel anger signs again, you must call for another Time Out. Take as many Time Outs as needed. A Time Out does not last for days; the duration should be anywhere from a half hour to two or three hours.

Explain the Time Out concept to your significant other if relevant or appropriate. Do this ahead of time to maximize a partner's cooperation with the exercise. Callers of Time Out should explain their responsibility for calling it and their responsibility for reconvening. Many arguments escalate when one person attempts to leave and the other stops him or follows him around. When a Time Out is called, all discussion is to stop immediately. The Time Out is not to be taken in a hostile way. There is to be no shouting. No doors are to be slammed on the way out. No last words are to be gotten in.

During the Time Out, do not think about what made you angry. This is like stewing and brewing. The thinking will only prolong the anger. Distract yourself from any thoughts related to the angering situation. This may have to be done again and again, since angry thoughts will tend to creep back in. There will be more on angry thoughts in a following chapter. Return when you think you can talk about your anger calmly, but, if anger escalates again, take another Time Out.

:60 Second Exercise: Scripting

Write a script for how you will implement a Time Out. What will you say? What will you do? How will you reconvene? How will you constructively deal with any problems, such as your partner not cooperating?

_____

_____

_____

_____

_____

_____

_____

_____

_____

_____

_____

_____

Another exercise is to practice taking a Time Out as a dry run. Engage in all aspects of the Time Out, from calling it to practicing a relaxing activity to reconvening. This way, when in the heat of the moment, you will know exactly what to do and where to go, as will your partner.

:60 Second Exercise: Time Out Dry Run

Write a review of your dry run Time Out exercise . What was said? What did you do? What did your partner do? How do you feel it went? What needs to be worked on? Get feedback from your partner. Take another dry run incorporating needed changes.

_____

_____

_____

_____

_____

_____

_____

_____

_____

_____

_____

_____

_____

When a formal Time Out technique is inconvenient or inappropriate, for example at work, mentally call a Time Out on yourself and engage in appropriate relaxing activities. This can simply mean anything from taking deep, slow, calming breaths to using imagery to take yourself to a nice, relaxing place. The techniques will be covered in detail in the next chapter.

If you are driving your car when anger is triggered, call a Time Out, pull over and exit the vehicle. Take a walk to calm yourself down. If you are in a car and cannot pull over to take a Time Out, you and your partner should cease all discussion. Relax and distract yourself from thoughts related to the anger; perhaps turn on the radio. Only resume the conversation when calm sets in and you feel cool enough to talk again.

If you are at home and cannot leave the house when you become angry, call a Time Out and go to another room. Ask your partner to respect this. Tell your partner you will return when you are calm.

If you commit to using this procedure consistently each and every time you feel signs of anger, you will end the instances of destructive anger expression. Do not deviate from this. Remember: the Time Out will always work if utilized correctly and consistently.

Anger internalizers also benefit from using the Time Out process. They notice their signs and cease brewing. They relax and return to express themselves calmly. This assertiveness will be discussed in a following chapter.

It is common for people to become complacent. I have seen it many times in my practice. A couple will avoid a few arguments by using the Time Out technique and then lapse back into not using it, because it seems easier. Real, permanent change is going to take hard work. The Time Out technique needs to be adhered to consistently until other techniques, to be discussed in later chapters, make it unnecessary. It should certainly be used as long as angry arguing is still occurring.

Some men may have trouble calling a Time Out. Men are trained in our society not to walk away. They may see this as weakness. Dispel and dispute those ideas. It takes strength to call a Time Out or walk away. The strength to exert self-control is more important than the false bravado of standing up to someone else or seeing an argument through to its negative conclusion.

:60 Second Exercise: Dispelling Myths

Write down any myths you hold on to which might make it hard for you to call a Time Out and walk away. Dispute each one.

1) _____

_____

_____

2) _____

_____

_____

3) _____

_____

_____

4) _____

_____

_____

Whereas women sometimes will call the police for help in the midst of an angry, out-of-control situation, men rarely do. It is better to call the police if being attacked by a partner than to strike back. In many cases of physical abuse, both partners act out physically. When the police are called, men are usually the ones arrested. Again, it is better to call the police before anger is acted out physically, even if it means your partner could go to jail. Men may feel ashamed doing this, but the laws protect them in the same way they protect women. If a man is scratched and bleeding or bruised and the woman is not, the woman may be the one that goes to jail. Usually, however, police who have been properly trained walk the individuals through a time-out-like technique. They separate the individuals and encourage them to talk it out. Then they bring the couple back together and attempt to help them resolve their conflict before an arrest is made. Referrals are given for help. If a party is under the influence of a substance, however, he or she is likely to be removed by the police. Arrests can actually be beneficial in that they usually lead to court-ordered treatment for either substance abuse, anger management or both. Victims are also referred to appropriate services. So don't be afraid that your partner will end up in prison. He or she may stay overnight in jail and then will see a judge and be ordered to get help. When necessary, call and cooperate with the police. They are trained to help.

:60 Second Exercise: Blowing the Whistle on Abuse

Write down any thoughts or attitudes you may have that would make you reluctant to call the police if your partner abuses you. Then dispute them.

Thoughts

1.) _____

_____

_____

2.) _____

_____

_____

3.) _____

_____

_____

Dispute Them

1.) _____

_____

_____

2.) _____

_____

_____

3.) _____

_____

_____

:60 Second Tips: Anger Emergency

♦ Use Time Out as a :60 Second emergency, stopgap procedure to avoid acting out of anger.

♦ Call a Time Out if you notice your anger cues.

♦ Remember, it is your responsibility to call a Time Out.

♦ Remove yourself from the situation and relax. Do not stew and brew.

♦ Return as soon as possible. Stay away no longer than a few hours.

♦ Check in with the other person if appropriate.

♦ Explain the Time Out concept to your partner ahead of time, not during an argument.

♦ Remember that you may take more than one Time Out.

♦ Practice a dry run.

♦ Know that Time Outs can be adapted to your place of work or other situations.

♦ If you or your partner is driving, cease all discussion.

♦ Stick to using the Time Out, keep to the rules and you will stop acting out in anger.

♦ Realize it is strong, not weak, to walk away.

♦ Call the police before destructive anger is expressed.

CHAPTER 9

If You Are Relaxed, You Cannot Possibly Be Angry

"Image creates desire. You will what you imagine."
-J. G. Gallimore

Relaxation and anger are antithetical responses. They involve different brain waves and other bodily reactions and so cannot possibly occur together. Research has shown the amazing ability of people to exert control over their bodies through such activities as meditation, self-hypnosis, biofeedback and relaxation training. For example, in biofeedback people are given readings about a body function such as heart rate or blood pressure. Simply by receiving audio or visual feedback, people have learned to slow their heart rates and lower their blood pressures. All of these techniques are variations of the same thing. They all increase the occurrence of alpha waves in the brain. Alpha waves are associated with states of deep relaxation. The bottom line is that relaxation training works. If you practice, you can become very effective at relaxation. In a short period of time, you can learn to relax by yourself almost immediately on cue. This will become a handy :60 Second skill not only for managing anger, but for improving your sense of well-being.

By practicing meditation, yoga, relaxation or even prayer, you can calm yourself. Transcendental Meditation, popular in the nineteen-sixties, was nothing more than repeating a mantra (your special word) in rhythm with your breathing. Studies have shown that the word "one" spoken in rhythm with breathing is equally as effective as formal Transcendental

Meditation in producing alpha waves and other measurable physiological indicators of relaxation such as lowered heart rate and a warming of the extremities (hands and feet).

The Reinforcing Cycle

Emotions, behaviors and thoughts all influence each other. In the field of psychology there is debate about which comes first, sort of like the argument over the chicken and the egg. All you need to know is that the cycle of feeling, thinking and acting drives and reinforces itself. You may think back to the last time you felt angry and realize that the more you thought about it, the angrier you became. This led to you acting on your anger, which may have dispelled some of it or achieved a purpose (although in a destructive way). Thus, the action was reinforced.

You can break that cycle. You *do* have control over your thoughts and your actions. By changing these, you can reduce your anger. In this chapter, we will discuss relaxation as a way of breaking the cycle of anger by intervening on the level of behavior. In the next chapter, we will discuss changing thoughts as a way of breaking the cycle.

Stress leads to tension. Tension can lead to agitation. Agitation can lead to anger. By reducing stress we can reduce the chance that we will become angry. One way is to replace negative coping mechanisms with positive ones. Most people cope successfully with 98 percent of their stressors. We make hundreds of adjustments each day and manage most situations quite well. Usually no single strategy will be effective in managing all of life's challenges. That is why we need a variety of coping skills or "copers." Most people use three or four favorite coping styles over and over again; these are copers they rely on regularly to get through most tough situations. Every one of their coping mechanisms works, or they wouldn't use them again. However, some copers have a high cost. We call these negative copers. Smoking, overeating and drinking do bring immediate relief from tension, but the positive effects don't last long and the negative side effects are often quite serious. Most negative copers are effective, short-term stress relievers, but they create additional problems if repeated over a long period of time or in response to many stressors.

NEGATIVE COPERS

ALCOHOL:	Drink to change your mood. Use alcohol as your friend.
DENIAL:	Pretend nothing is wrong. Lie. Ignore the problem.
DRUGS:	Abuse coffee/aspirin/medications. Smoke pot. Pop pills.
EATING:	Binge. Go on constant diets or use food to console you.
FAULT-FINDING:	Have a judgmental attitude. Complain. Criticize.
ILLNESS:	Develop headaches/nervous stomach/major illness. Become accident prone.
INDULGING:	Stay up late. Sleep in. Buy on impulse. Waste time.
PASSIVITY:	Hope it gets better. Procrastinate. Wait for a lucky break.
REVENGE:	Be sarcastic. Talk mean. Get even.
STUBBORNNESS:	Be rigid. Demand your way. Refuse to be wrong.
TANTRUMS:	Yell. Mope. Pout. Swear. Drive recklessly.
TOBACCO:	Smoke to relieve tension.
WITHDRAWAL:	Avoid the situation. Skip school or work. Keep your feelings to yourself.
WORRYING:	Fret over things. Imagine the worst.

:60 Second Exercise: Identify Negative Copers

Identify your negative copers. Write down what these copers do for you and what they "cost" you.

Negative Coper	What it does for you	What it costs you
1)_____	_____	_____
2)_____	_____	_____
3)_____	_____	_____
4)_____	_____	_____
5)_____	_____	_____
6)_____	_____	_____

POSITIVE COPERS

Positive Copers are those techniques that are reliable, positive stress relievers without the negative side effects. These skills can be used over and over again for a variety of stressful situations.

DIVERSIONS

GETAWAYS:	Spend time alone. See a movie. Daydream.
HOBBIES:	Write. Paint. Remodel. Create something.
LEARNING:	Take a class. Read. Join a club.
MUSIC:	Play an instrument. Sing. Listen to the stereo.
PLAY:	Play a game. Go out with friends. Take up a sport.
WORK:	Tackle a new project. Keep busy. Volunteer.

FAMILY

BALANCING:	Balance time at work and home. Accept the good with the bad.
CONFLICT RESOLUTION:	Look for win/win solutions. Forgive readily.
ESTEEM-BUILDING:	Build good family feelings. Focus on personal strengths.

FLEXIBILITY: Take on new family roles. Be open to change.

NETWORKING: Develop friendships with other families. Make use of community resources.

TOGETHERNESS: Take time to be together. Build family traditions. Express affection.

INTERPERSONAL

AFFIRMATION: Believe in yourself. Trust others. Give compliments.

ASSERTIVENESS: State your needs and wants. Say "no" respectfully.

CONTACT: Make new friends. Touch. Really listen to others.

EXPRESSION: Show feelings. Share thoughts.

LIMITS: Accept others' boundaries.

LINKING: Share problems with others.

MENTAL

IMAGINATION: Look for the humor in life. Anticipate the future.

LIFE PLANNING: Set clear goals. Plan for the future.

ORGANIZING: Take charge. Make order. Don't let things pile up.

PROBLEM-SOLVING: Solve it yourself. Seek outside help. Tackle problems head on.

RELABELING: Change perspectives. Look for good in a bad situation.

TIME MANAGEMENT: Focus on top priorities. Work smarter, not harder.

PHYSICAL

FITNESS: Walk. Exercise. Play physical games.

VALUING: Set priorities. Be consistent. Spend time and energy wisely.

DIET: Eat a balanced diet including plenty of fresh fruits and vegetables. Don't overeat.

SPIRITUAL

COMMITMENT: Take up a worthy cause. Say "yes." Invest yourself meaningfully.

FAITH: Find purpose and meaning. Trust God.

PRAYER: Confess. Ask forgiveness. Pray for others. Give thanks.

SURRENDER: Let go of problems. Learn to live with the situation.

WORSHIP: Share beliefs with others. Put faith into action.

:60 Second Exercise: Future Copers

Write down one or two copers that you do not use now, but that you think might be the most effective additions to your repertoire of coping skills.

1) _____

2) _____

:60 Second Exercise: Time Management

Effective time management contributes to a balanced lifestyle. Review the following list and choose some time management tips that you can incorporate into your life to accomplish more and feel less stressed. Check off the ones you will use.

☐ Be realistic with yourself regarding how much you can actually accomplish in a given span of time.

☐ Say "NO" to additional responsibilities that infringe on personal, leisure or work time.

☐ Prioritize your tasks, because they are not equally important. Set priorities on a daily, weekly and monthly basis for maximizing accomplishments.

☐ Develop an awareness of your peak energy period of the day and plan to do activities with the highest energy demand at that time.

☐ Review what the best use of your time is currently on a regular basis.

☐ Complete tasks well enough to get the results that you really need. Striving for perfection is generally not necessary and can burn up time better spent in another way.

☐ Delegate tasks and responsibilities to others whenever appropriate. Be sure to communicate your expectations clearly.

☐ Don't waste time thinking and rethinking decisions for basic issues. Make those decisions quickly and move on.

☐ Approach difficult tasks that you are not looking forward to with a positive attitude. You will be surprised at how much stress that can relieve.

☐ Break big, overwhelming tasks into small, manageable ones. That way it's easier to keep track of your progress and achievements.

☐ Be prepared to make good use of "waiting" time by having small tasks or activities to do. Another alternative is to always be prepared to take advantage of potential relaxation time when there are no demands on you.

☐ Request time when you need it to focus on your goals without interruption. Take time to create a conducive work environment at home and at work.

☐ Set goals and reward yourself when you have accomplished them. If it is a big goal, you may want to build in small rewards at certain milestones.

☐ Remind yourself from time to time how good it feels to accomplish a task, what the benefits of accomplishment are and the relief of having that weight off your shoulders.

☐ Build in time for self-care, leisure activities and exercise, as well as completing necessary tasks. Remember, taking care of yourself is also a priority.

:60 Second Review: Proven Stress Reducers

1. Get up fifteen minutes earlier in the morning. The inevitable morning mishaps will be less stressful.

2. Don't rely on your memory. Write down appointment times, when to pick up the laundry, when library books are due, etc. As an old Chinese proverb wisely states, "The palest ink is better than the most retentive memory."

3. Remember, procrastination is stressful. Whatever you want to do tomorrow, do *today*. Whatever you want to do today, do it *now*.

4. Plan ahead: Don't let the gas tank get below one-quarter full, keep a well stocked "emergency shelf" of staples at home, don't wait until

you're down to your last bus token or postage stamp to buy more, etc.

5. Don't put up with something that does not work right. If your alarm clock, coffeemaker, shoelaces, windshield wipers—whatever—are constant sources of aggravation, get them fixed or get new ones.

6. Be prepared to wait. A paperback book can make a wait in a post office line seem fairly quick and quite pleasant.

7. Remember Pollyanna! For every one thing that goes wrong, there are probably ten or fifty or one hundred blessings. Count 'em!

8. Turn "needs" into *preferences*. Our basic physical needs translate into food, water and keeping warm. Everything else is a preference. Don't get attached to preferences.

9. Simplify, simplify, simplify.

10. Make friends with non-worriers. Nothing can get you into the habit of worrying faster than associating with chronic worrywarts.

11. Create order out of chaos. Organize your home and work space so that you always know exactly where things are. Put things away where they belong and you won't have to go through the stress of losing things.

12. Add an ounce of love to everything you do.

13. Become more flexible. Some things are *not* worth doing perfectly and some issues are fine to compromise upon.

14. Eliminate destructive self-talk. "I'm too old to...," "I'm too fat to...," etc.

15. "Worry about the pennies and the dollars will take care of themselves." That's another way of saying take care of the things you can take care of today and the big things of tomorrow will still be there tomorrow; don't fret over them!

16. Do one thing at a time. When you are with someone, be with that person and let no one or nothing else interfere. When you are busy with a project, concentrate on doing *that* project and forget about everything else you have to do.

17. Do especially unpleasant tasks early in the day and get them over with. Then the rest of your day will be free of anxiety.

18. Learn to delegate responsibility to others who you believe are capable.

19. Forget about counting to ten. Count to *one thousand* before doing something or saying anything that could make matters worse.
20. Adopt a forgiving view of events and people. Accept that we all are imperfect beings living in an imperfect world.

You can add to your repertoire of relaxing activities by learning a formal relaxation method. I will explain a number of relaxation techniques and guide you step-by-step through each. You will be given exercises to practice these techniques. One can become better and better at relaxing by practicing. Relaxation is a powerful tool to reduce stress in general and to reduce anger when early warning signs are noticed. All of us can benefit by practicing relaxation either twenty minutes a day or in shorter sessions throughout the day as stress accumulates. The techniques can also be used for the purpose of aiding sleep. You can start your relaxation by thinking to yourself, *I will relax just for the sake of relaxing,* or you can think, *I will relax for the purpose of falling asleep.* Such auto-suggestions will increase your positive expectations about and responses to relaxation. It is also important to distinguish for yourself why you are relaxing.

As I guide my patients through relaxation techniques, I usually make audiotapes of the exercises. They take the tapes home to assist in their practices. In the beginning this makes it easier to focus. Later on, as the techniques become more familiar to them, they do not need to use the tapes. You can learn the techniques without a tape. If you prefer, many libraries and bookstores have audiotape relaxation exercises. Try to find one that has more than just relaxing sounds like waves, rain or soft music. There are also subliminal tapes to help relaxation, which involve inaudible suggestions. I recommend that you look for an audiotape that runs you through an actual relaxation technique. The purpose is to reach a point where you are able to relax yourself without the need for a written or taped exercise. Usually, after about three weeks of practice you will be at the point where you can relax quickly on your own.

Next, I will give you a script of a full relaxation exercise. An alternative to a commercially produced audiotape is to make your own recording of the exercise. Since many people feel uncomfortable listening to their own voices, ask someone else to tape the exercise for you. The person should speak in a soft, soothing voice and go slowly, reading as he or she breathes out naturally. This is what I do when I make a tape for someone. I always end up relaxing myself too, because I follow along with the exercise as I speak it. Since different parts of the relaxation exercise work better for different people, I often re-record a tape emphasizing the parts that work best for the individual. That is why I make individual tapes with people in session as I watch them respond to the exercise. An exercise can be tailored for the individual. As you practice, emphasize what works for you. As you read and practice the exercise, go slowly. Read to yourself as you breathe out naturally.

Do you remember C.A.R.E. from chapter 1? "R" is for relaxation response. There are a number of :60 Second relaxation techniques reviewed there. What will follow now will be a fifteen to twenty minute exercise incorporating all aspects of relaxation. The technique is to be practiced in full at first. However, it is broken into three phases. The first focuses on muscle tension and relaxation. It helps to become aware of the difference between the bad feelings of tension and the good feelings of relaxation. The second phase involves placing oneself in a relaxing place in every sense. This is achieved through the use of imagery. The third phase involves a countdown, where we count from ten down to zero. With each number we focus on becoming more and more relaxed. If you are practicing for the sake of relaxation, when you get to zero you will open your eyes feeling relaxed and refreshed. If you are practicing to help yourself get to sleep, you can keep your eyes closed and allow yourself to drift off to sleep. This is not difficult, because you will probably be asleep by then anyway. Invariably, in my office, patients fall asleep before we get through the full exercise. When they use the tape to relax or practice, they tell me they never hear the end of the tape, because they are sleeping by then. That is okay, because if you fall asleep, you must be pretty relaxed.

The reason for the three phases is that after one week of practicing, you will be ready to skip Phase I. After two weeks you can drop Phase II. After three weeks you'll be able to relax on cue by blowing or breathing out and letting your muscles relax as you imagine draining tension down and out of your body. Within three weeks of practice you should be able to relax in :60 Seconds or less.

Relaxation Training

Relaxation should be practiced in a quiet place with the lights turned down low. There are to be no interruptions, so pick a good time like after the kids are asleep, the dog is walked and your partner is absorbed in an activity in another room. Remove yourself from potential distractions: turn off the television, stereo, computer, video game system, electric popcorn popper, pager, cell phone, sonic jewelry cleaner, etc. Let the answering machine or computer voicemail system pick up the phone calls.

We will begin with Phase I of the relaxation exercise. You may relax while lying down or sitting in a comfortable chair. Try to use as few muscles as possible to hold yourself in your position. You can relax just for the sake of relaxing or to help fall asleep. If you are comfortable doing it, close your eyes. This alone increases your sense of relaxation. If you prefer, keep your eyes open and fix your gaze on one point. After a while your eyes may feel heavy and tired and it will feel good to just let them close. Letting whatever thoughts come up just flow in and out of your mind. Don't focus on anything in particular, just the good feelings of relaxation. Note the difference between tension in your muscles and relaxation in your muscles. Let any background sounds increase your sense of relaxation. Draw your attention now to the muscles of the top of your head, forehead, face and throat. If you feel any tension in any of these muscles, first notice it and then just relax it away. Melt it away. Imagine the tension draining down, out of your head and face and exiting the tip of your chin. Practice deep, even breathing. Notice the difference between tense feelings and relaxing feelings.

Now draw your attention to the muscles of the back of your neck. This is a place where we hold much tension. Notice any tension in those muscles. Then relax the tension away. Just drain the tension out of your neck muscles. Imagine that the cushion under your head is like a large sponge that is soaking the tension out of your neck muscles. Notice the difference between the bad feelings of tension and the good feelings of relaxation.

Now focus your attention on your right shoulder. This is another place where we hold much tension. Notice any tension in your right shoulder muscles. Move it around a little to let the tension go. Drain tension down, out of your right shoulder. Imagine the tension flowing down through your right arm. Let the tension drain down through your biceps, past the elbow, through your lower arm, past the wrist, through your hand and imagine it passing out through the tips of your fingers. Notice the feeling of relaxation in your right arm. Continue your deep, even breathing. Feel calm and peaceful, quiet and relaxed.

And now, focus on your left shoulder. Notice any tension in your left shoulder muscles. Drain the tension down and out of your left arm, just letting it go out the tips of your fingers. Enjoy the relaxing feelings.

Become aware now of the rhythm of your breathing. Feel the air as it comes in and goes out. Don't control your breathing, just breath naturally. Nice and even. Realize that breathing is an automatic reflex; you do not even have to think about breathing. It is a natural body process. Clean the toxins out of your lungs, bring in fresh, cleansing air. Feel the air as it passes through your nostrils all the way down to the pit of your stomach. And as you breathe out, imagine that just as you are releasing toxins you are also releasing tension. With each breath out, you are blowing more and more tension out of your body. With each breath out, you are becoming more and more relaxed. Feel your chest rising and falling with the rhythm of your breathing. Notice any tension in the muscles of your chest. Use the breathing now to melt the tension away. Use your breath to relax tension out of your chest muscles. Notice the difference between tension and relaxation. Practice nice, even breathing. Feel calm and peaceful, quiet and relaxed.

Now focus your attention on the muscles of your stomach. Notice any tension and drain the tension away. Relax the tension away. Just blow the tension out with each breath you exhale. Feel the relaxation building with each breath you inhale. And as you breathe in you might say to yourself, *Calm*, and as you breathe out you might say, *Peace. Calm... Peace... Calm... Peace...* Say it in rhythm with your breathing. And just by repeating the words calm and peace you are deepening your sense of relaxation. Focus on the words calm and peace as your breath comes in and goes out. Let whatever thoughts come to mind come in and go out. Don't focus on anything in particular, just the relaxation exercise, the rhythm of your breathing and the words calm as you breathe in and peace as you breathe out. *Calm... Peace... Calm... Peace... Calm... Peace...*

Focus your attention on the muscles in your upper back. If you feel any tension there, take note of it and then drain it away. Imagine that whatever you are lying on is a big sponge soaking the tension out of the muscles of your upper back. Now focus on your lower back, another place where we hold much tension. Pay particular attention to this area if you have back problems. Notice any tension there and let it melt away. Drain it away with the rhythm of your breathing. Notice the difference between the tense feelings and discomfort and the pleasant, relaxed feelings as the tension dissipates. Relax those muscles more and more with each breath you exhale. Feel calm and peaceful, quiet and relaxed.

Now if you notice any tension has built back up in any of the muscles of the head, face, neck, shoulders, arms, hands, fingers, chest, stomach or upper and lower back, draw your attention to it and relax it away. Move the muscles slightly to relax them. That's right...Very good. Notice tension and let it drain away. Blow it out of your body with each breath out. Feel more and more deeply relaxed with each breath out. Feel calm and peaceful, quiet and relaxed.

Draw your attention to the muscles of your right buttock and upper thigh. Drain the tension down and out. Notice the difference between tense feelings and relaxed feelings in the muscles of the right buttock and upper thigh. Notice any tension there and drain it down through your leg, past your knee, through your calf, past your ankle, through your foot and imagine letting it go out through the tips of your toes. Drain the tension down and out. Notice the difference between tense feelings and relaxed feelings in the muscles of the right leg.

And now focus on the left leg. Notice any tension and relax it away. Drain the tension down and out of your leg. Let it go out through the tips of your toes. Blow the tension out with each breath you exhale. Continue your deep, even breathing. Feel calm and peaceful, quiet and relaxed.

All the muscles in your body should now feel relaxed. If you notice any lingering tension in any of your muscles, focus on that area and try to relax the tension away. Consciously drain it out of the muscle. You may feel warm or cool, heavy or light. You may feel tingly. Just go with whatever you are feeling. Do not focus on anything in particular. Focus only on the good feelings of relaxation and the rhythm of your breathing. Now you are relaxed from the top of your head to the tips of your toes. Learn to notice tension and relax it away. Notice the difference between tense feelings and relaxed feelings. End Phase I now, as physically relaxed as can be. And as you relax on the outside, relax on the inside as well.

Do not move. Stay very physically relaxed as we begin Phase II of the relaxation exercise. Realize that a picture is like a thousand words. Place yourself now in a relaxing scene. Imagine yourself lying on a soft blanket in the middle of a grassy field in the country. Feel the blanket under your body and the ground cradling you so that you do not have to move even a single muscle to hold yourself in position. Feel the warm sun on your skin and a cooling breeze brush over you keeping your temperature just right. Look straight up and see the blue sky and some white, puffy clouds. Birds are circling in the thermals way overhead. The trees that surround the field sway in the breeze. See the rolling, grassy field with wild flowers growing here and there. Notice the different shades of green of the trees, shrubs and grass. Hear the sound of the breeze gently rustling the leaves of the trees. There is a small brook somewhere in the distance. Hear the cool water gurgling as it tumbles over the rocks. Hear the sound of the birds singing and insects chirping. Smell the fresh country air as you breathe it in and out. Smell the fresh cold water of the brook. The air is so clean and fresh you can almost taste the purity of it. Remain in this relaxing place. Realize that you can return to this relaxing place whenever you need to and whenever you want to. Just by placing yourself here in every sense, you can increase relaxation. Experience the sensations, sights, sounds, smells and even the tastes of this relaxing place. Find it easier and easier to place yourself here each time you return. Find the motivation to practice relaxing each time you return.

Stay in that relaxing place and remain still. We will now begin Phase III of the relaxation exercise: the countdown. Count down from ten to zero. With each number that you count, feel yourself become more and more relaxed, more and more at peace.

TEN: If you notice any tension in any muscle of your body relax it away. Just blow the tension out of the muscle with each breath out.

NINE: Feel the air as it comes in and goes out. It passes through your nostrils, all the way down to your diaphragm. With each breath out, feel more and more deeply relaxed, more and more at peace.

EIGHT: As you breathe say, *Calm* and *Peace. Calm... Peace... Calm... Peace... Calm... Peace...*

SEVEN: Feel the warm sun on your skin and the cool breeze brushing over you.

SIX: See the blue sky, white puffy clouds and birds circling way overhead.

FIVE: Hear the sound of the leaves rustling gently in the cool breeze, the sound of the shallow water tumbling over the rocks, the bird songs.

FOUR: Smell the fresh country air as you breathe it in and out. It's so clean and pure you can almost taste it. And with each breath you exhale, you are becoming more and more relaxed and very removed from your surroundings. You are away, off in the distance somewhere and very deeply involved in your relaxation.

THREE: If you notice any tension, melt it away with the rhythm of your breathing. Let it drain out of your body into the ground beneath you, as though the ground were a huge sponge, soaking all tension out of your muscles.

TWO: You are very deeply relaxed now. Enjoy the relaxing feelings and your deep, even breathing. Feel calm and peaceful, quiet and relaxed.

ONE: You are completely relaxed now. Realize that this is a place to which you can return any time you need to or want to. Find it easier and easier each time you try to achieve a state of deep relaxation. Find the energy and motivation to achieve your goal. You are relaxed, open and receptive. Use this state to become the person you want to be: a person able to achieve his goals, able to let go of tension and anger, able to calmly express her feelings. Feel good about how you think, feel and behave. Feel good about yourself. Accept yourself.

When we get to zero, you can remain relaxed and drift off to sleep if you like. If you are just relaxing, you can open your eyes, feeling relaxed and refreshed. Retain now what you experienced during this relaxation exercise and you will find it easier and easier to return each time you try. Feel the air now as you breathe in. With each breath in, feel the energy pulsing into your body. Become more aware of your surroundings.

ZERO.

This is the end of the exercise. Remember, it is best to practice once each day or every other day. Each week you can eliminate a Phase. First eliminate Phase I, then II and finally just use Phase III, which incorporates all of the techniques of the other Phases. Realize that by practicing, you can get to the point where you are just using the countdown. Your ability to relax can become so highly developed that you will be able to relax on cue. Notice tension. Let it go. Be aware of your breathing and then take a few relaxing breaths out. Imagine yourself in a relaxing place. Thus, you have achieved a :60 Second skill to relax yourself.

As you practice you may replace the relaxation scene suggested in the exercise with others of your own choice. You might place yourself on a beach or in a hammock swinging between two trees. One patient liked to return to her childhood bedroom at her grandparents' house. Lying in bed, she experienced all of the sensations, sights, sounds, smells and tastes of relaxing in a comfortable bed in that quiet and safe room, from hearing the comforting sounds of her grandparents in the house to smelling delicious food cooking in the kitchen.

:60 Second Exercise: Relaxation

Write down one or two especially relaxing places where you have been in your life, special places that you have long remembered. These should be places you can let yourself go to in your mind's eye. Place yourself there as was done in Phase II. Visit these special scenes when you are practicing or when you need to relax.

Describe the first place in every detail:

1) Sensations_____

_____

_____

_____

2) Sights _____

_____

_____

_____

3) Sounds _____

_____

_____

_____

4) Smells _____

_____

_____

_____

5) Tastes _____

_____

_____

_____

Describe the second place in every detail:

1) Sensations_____

_____

_____

_____

2) Sights _____

_____

_____

_____

3) Sounds _____

_____

_____

_____

4) Smells _____

_____

_____

_____

5) Tastes _____

_____

_____

_____

:60 Second Rating Scale

When you practice the relaxation exercise it is a good idea to do a simple rating of your level of tension before you begin and then your level of tension right after the exercise. Use a five-point rating scale, five being the most tense or angry you have ever been and one being the most relaxed you have ever been. Circle the number that you feel is appropriate for your level of tension/anger or relaxation. Following that, describe some of the emotions you experienced. Try this on several occasions.

Date: _____

Before Relaxation Exercise: 5   4   3   2   1

After Relaxation Exercise: 5   4   3   2   1

Emotions Experienced: _____

_____

Date: _____

Before Relaxation Exercise: 5   4   3   2   1

After Relaxation Exercise: 5   4   3   2   1

Emotions Experienced: _____

_____

Date: _____

Before Relaxation Exercise: 5   4   3   2   1

After Relaxation Exercise: 5   4   3   2   1

Emotions Experienced: _____

_____

By using this scale you can keep track of the effect of the relaxation exercise. It will help reinforce its use when you see that before the exercise you felt you were at 5 or 4 on the scale and that after the exercise, you went down to 2 or 1.

There is a variation on Phase I of the exercise. The one already described in previous pages is called Progressive Muscle Relaxation. The other technique that can be implemented for Phase I is called

Jacobsonian Relaxation (named for the man who developed it). This method may be preferable to people who like a more active technique. They might find it easier to pay attention to this exercise as it gives them more to do. If you have any orthopedic or muscle problems, however, you should check with your doctor about using it or modify the exercise so that you do not strain or injure your body.

Jacobsonian Relaxation Exercise Alternative

Remove your glasses and shoes and get into a comfortable position on a bed or in a chair. We will go through each of the major muscle groups of the body. We will first tense the muscles for five counts and then relax the muscles for ten counts. Let's begin.

First, focus on the muscles of your head and face: knit your brow, squeeze your eyes shut tightly, wrinkle up your nose and tense your mouth and cheeks. Hold it... Feel the muscles tightening. Notice the tension building... Tighten it... Hold it... Now relax... Feel the tension draining out of the muscles... Just let it go... Notice the difference between the tension and the relaxation. Enjoy the relaxing feeling for ten seconds.

Next we'll work on the muscles of the back of your neck. Push back against the cushion or pillow... Compress your neck muscles... Feel the tension building... Hold it... Tighten it... Hold it... Now relax... Feel the tension draining. Enjoy the good feeling of the relaxation for ten seconds.

Now we'll go on to the muscles of your shoulders and upper back. Hunch up your shoulders... Tighten the muscles... Feel the tension building... Hold it... Tighten it... Hold it... That's right... Now relax... Let the tension drain out of your shoulders and upper back muscles. Feel it draining away. Notice the feeling of relaxing the muscles. You are becoming better and better at noticing the difference between tense feelings and relaxed feelings in your muscles.

Now let's focus on the lower back. Arch your back and tighten those muscles... Build the tension... Hold it... Hold it... Now relax... Feel the tension draining away. Enjoy the relaxation in the muscles of your lower back.

Now think about your chest: Tighten the pectoral muscles... Hold it... Tighten it... Feel the tension... Now relax... Let it go. Feel the difference as the tension drains.

Now shift your attention to your stomach muscles. Tighten your abdominal muscles as though you were preparing to take a punch... Tighten... Hold... Hold... Relax... Notice and enjoy the relaxed feelings in your stomach.

Next, focus on your right buttock. Squeeze the muscle... Hold it... Tighten it... Hold it... Now relax. Focus on the difference between tension and relaxation. Learn to recognize the feeling of tension so that you can let it go.

Now concentrate on the left buttock. Tighten the muscle... Feel the tension build... Hold... Tighten... Hold... Now relax. Enjoy the feeling of relaxation.

Next, move to your right thigh. Tighten those muscles... Hold it... Build the tension... Hold it... Now relax. Notice the difference.

Now think about your left thigh. Squeeze the tension... Hold it... Tighten it... Hold it... Now relax. Feel the tension drain away.

Now arch your right foot up and tense the right calf. Hold it... Tighten the muscles... Build the tension... Hold it... Relax. Notice the difference.

Now work on the left side. Arch your foot... Tighten your left calf... Hold it... Build the tension... Hold it... Now relax... Let it go. Enjoy the feeling of relaxation in your left calf muscle and foot.

Now move to the toes on your right foot. Curl your toes under and build the tension... Hold... Tighten... Hold... Relax. Notice the difference.

Last, think about the toes on your left foot. Curl your toes under. Tighten the muscles... Hold it... Build the tension... Relax. Be aware of the sensation of relaxation and the difference between the tight, tense muscles and the relaxed, loose ones.

Lie still now and let go of all tension. Be aware of it, then relax it away. Loosen all your muscles from the top of your head to your toes. You should feel totally physically relaxed now. You can use this exercise to become more aware of tension in your muscles so that you can actively relax it away. Know that a picture is worth a thousand words and while you relax on the outside you relax on the inside as well.

The neck area is especially vulnerable to tension. Many of us hold a great deal of tension in our necks. We walk around all day not even recognizing the tension building until our necks are throbbing. As a psychologist, I spend all day listening to what people say. If I do not listen and truly understand what they are expressing, thinking and feeling, I cannot even begin to help them. When one listens carefully, what needs to be done as a therapist becomes very clear. However, at the same time, there is a subconscious tendency when listening intently to arch the head forward with chin protruding. This puts pressure on the muscles of the back of the neck. After a number of hours one can feel real pain in that area.

While serving an internship, a supervisor asked me if I had neck aches. He pointed out that I had "listener's neck." As much as I try to pay attention to this, put my head back and tuck in my chin, there are days when my neck really aches by 8:00 P.M. By focusing on this one area and using the exercises described in this chapter, I can quickly relax myself. If you suffer from a tense, achy neck, you too can achieve this relaxation. When you do not have time to go through the complete set of relaxation exercises, you can do one :60 Second exercise focused specifically on the muscles of the neck and surrounding areas. As you use these exercises you will notice that you not only are easing the tension in your neck, but that you feel more relaxed in general. Use these quick techniques to take your attention away from anything that is angering you.

:60 Second Exercises: Neck Stress Reduction

These exercises can be done at your desk, at home, in transit or just about any time. Go through each one slowly. Stretch gently and do not bounce your head.

ACTIVE NECK ROTATION

By relaxing your middle and upper neck muscles, this exercise increases flexibility for head-turning activities.

➢ **Don't force any motion. Go only as far as you can comfortably.**

1) Lie on your back with your knees bent and your feet flat on the floor. For extra comfort, place a neck roll or a rolled up towel under your neck.

2) Turn your head slowly from left to right, keeping your chin level. Repeat at least five times to each side, bringing your head back to the neutral position between each turn.

*Quick Tip: As a stretching challenge, rotate your legs and lower body in the opposite direction of your head and neck. Repeat five times in each direction.

FACE CLOCK

This exercise increases your neck mobility for front-facing activities.

➤ **Don't stay in one position too long. Keep your neck moving to avoid tightening your muscles.**

1) Lie on your back with your head in the neutral position, your knees and your feet flat on the floor.

2) Imagine you are facing a clock. Slowly trace the outer edge of the clock with the tip of your nose. Go clockwise first, then counter-clockwise. Repeat five times in each direction.

   *Quick Tip: At work, sitting at your desk, do the Face Clock on your breaks, after lunch and before you go home. Sit up straight with your back pressed firmly against your chair for extra support.

NECK FLEX

By stretching the muscles between your shoulder blades and at the base of your skull, the neck flex relaxes areas that get stiff.

➤ **Don't force your head down. Pull slowly, letting gravity help.**

1) Sit up straight in a chair. For more support, pull your left arm behind you and rest your left forearm against your lower back. Place your right palm on the back of your neck.

2) Gently pull your head forward and down, without forcing it. Hold for ten seconds. Return to neutral and repeat five times.

TENSION RELEASE

This exercise loosens the upper neck and shoulder muscles that often tighten with stress.

➤ **Don't overstretch. STOP if you feel pain or tingling.**

1) Sit up straight in your chair. Tuck your chin in slightly and tilt your head to the left, so your left ear is close to your left shoulder and your chin is down and pointing toward the right.

2) Reaching your left arm over your head, place your left hand on the upper right side of your head and gently pull your head toward

your left shoulder. Hold for ten seconds, then return to the neutral position. Repeat three times. Switch sides and do this exercise three more times.

*Quick tip: For even greater relaxation, breathe in deeply through your nose as your tilt your head. Then exhale through your mouth as you pull on your head.

REACH AND PULL

This exercise helps relieve tension between your shoulder blades and across your chest.

➢ **Don't force your elbows too far back if it feels like it's cramping your muscles.**

1) Reach forward with both arms extended straight out and parallel to the floor. Clasp your hands and lower your chin toward your chest. Round your shoulders, feeling the stretch between your shoulder blades. Hold for five seconds.

2) Unclasp your hands and return your head to neutral. With palms facing forward, bend your elbows and bring your forearms back until your elbows are behind you and your palms are past your ears. Push your chest out in front of you. Feel the stretch in your chest muscles. Return to the starting position and repeat both steps five times.

SHOULDER STRETCH

By increasing flexibility in your neck and upper back, the shoulder stretch helps you with pushing, pulling and reaching activities.

1) Raise your arms straight out to your sides until they're at shoulder height and parallel to the floor. Bend your arms up at the elbows, so your hands are a little above the height of your head. Don't let your upper arms or elbows drop below shoulder height.

2) Make relaxed fists and pull your forearms together in front of you until they touch. Round your shoulders and feel the stretch between your shoulder blades. Hold for ten seconds. Slowly return to the starting position. Repeat ten times.

*Quick Tip: As a stretching challenge, bend your left arm in front of you and hold it with your right hand, just below the elbow. Pull your left elbow across the front of your body. Hold for five seconds and then switch sides. Repeat five times on each side.

PALM PRESS

The Palm Press develops strength in your upper and lower neck muscles, helping you with stationary activities.

➤ **Don't press so hard that you cause pain or your head shakes. Don't let your neck arch in any direction.**

1) Sit up straight. Leave your head in the neutral position. Press the palm of either hand against your forehead. Push slowly while resisting with your neck muscles, so your head does not move. Hold for five second, then slowly relax the pressure. Repeat five times.

2) Repeat the exercise, pressing five times on both the left side and the right side of your head.

3) Repeat the exercise, pressing five times on the back of your head.

HEAD LIFTS

Good for maintaining or regaining your range of motion, Head Lifts strengthen your upper neck muscles and improve flexibility.

➤ **Don't strain your neck by lifting your head above the level of your back.**

1) Lie on your back with knees bent and feet flat on the floor. Tuck in your chin and lift your head toward your chest, keeping your shoulders on the floor. Hold for five seconds and repeat ten times.

2) Turn onto your right side, resting your head on your right forearm. Lift your head slowly toward your left shoulder. Hold for five seconds and return to original position. Repeat ten times. Switch to your left side and repeat the exercise.

3) Get on your hands and knees, looking down at the floor. Keeping your back straight, let your head slowly drop toward your chest. Tuck in your chin, then lift your head until your neck is level with your back. Hold for five seconds then slowly drop your head again. Repeat ten times.

ARM LIFTS

By strengthening lower neck, shoulder and back muscles, Arm Lifts help you do lifting and reaching activities.

> ➢ **Don't let your head slip out of the neutral position; keep your ears in line with your shoulders and hips.**

1) Stand with a straight back, keeping your head and neck in the neutral position.

2) Alternate raising your arms out to your sides and up over your head with lowering them back to your sides. All the while keep your arms straight and moving in unison. Move in slow, smooth arcs. Repeat ten times.

REACH AND HOLD

This exercise develops strength and control in your neck, shoulder and back muscles, building endurance.

1) Get on your hands and knees, with knees spread hip-width distance apart. Keeping your head in the neutral position, tighten your abdominal muscles and raise your right arm straight out in front of you. Hold for five seconds, then lower your arm. Repeat five times, then do the same movement using your left arm.

2) Repeat the exercise, lifting your arm out to the side instead of the front. Raise each arm five times.

3) Now repeat the exercise, lifting your arm behind you. Raise each arm five times.

Your homework is to practice the full relaxation exercise—Phase I, II and III—every day or every other day for one week. After that week elapses, continue doing the relaxation exercise, but drop Phase I. After a full week of just doing Phases II and III, drop phase II so that the third week is spent doing only Phase III. Rate your tension level before and after each exercise.

Of course, you can use the techniques at any time when needed. At first, try to use the full exercise whenever you need it to derail anger. Later, you can find what works best for you to keep stress and anger at low and manageable levels.

:60 Second Tips: Relaxation

♦ Remember relaxation and anger cannot coexist at the same time.

♦ Know that you can control such things as your pulse, skin temperature and blood pressure with relaxation exercises.

♦ Manage your stress and anger with relaxation exercises.

♦ Break the feeling, thinking, behaving cycle of anger by relaxing.

♦ Use the exercises to create relaxation or aid sleep.

♦ Audiotapes assist training.

♦ Practice Progressive Muscle Relaxation or Jacobsonian Relaxation—whichever works best for you.

♦ Use the Relaxation Exercise involving three Phases: muscle relaxation, imagery and the countdown.

♦ As time passes and you become more skilled, you can drop Phases I and II.

♦ Rate your tension level before and after you use the exercises.

CHAPTER 10

Thinking about One Thing at a Time

"Knowing is not enough; we must apply.
Willing is not enough; we must do."
-Johann von Goethe

Believe it or not, the human brain is wired in such a way that it is impossible for us to think of more than one thing at a time. When I tell this to my patients, many are skeptical at first. One person in particular comes to mind. Susan was a nurse with twenty-five years of experience. She was highly intelligent and well trained in her field. She tended to have repetitive, rapid-fire thoughts which led to a number of unpleasant emotions including sadness and anger. It was hard for her to believe that she could only think about one thing at a time, because she tended to shift back and forth from one thought to another so rapidly. Susan, though, had come to me because her anger and depression were spiraling out of control, so we practiced taking control of her thoughts. Although it was difficult, she learned to reorient herself away from unpleasant memories and thoughts and her stress did reduce. She hoped it would become even easier to apply this technique and, over time and with much practice, it did.

In the beginning, however, Susan had hoped for a magical "cure" which would eliminate all bad feelings immediately. Unfortunately, in mental health there are no magical cures. There is guidance toward learning new skills for coping with and managing unhappiness, problems and anger. This takes hard work, mental effort and persistence, as you are probably realizing with what you've read and done already to improve your anger management skills. The effort and persistence is worthwhile. I have seen many people turn their lives around with guidance and joint effort.

I have used this technique to create awareness of the fact that we can only think of one thing at a time to help to control our negative thoughts. We all experience times when we are totally involved in the moment, in the activity or thoughts in which we are engaged. These tend to be rare and as soon as they are recognized they are usually lost, because our attention and concentration have wandered. Such moments have been described as "peak" experiences and are to be cherished and sought after. For example, time seems to go by quicker because I am not aware of it when I am completely engaged in and intensely concentrating on working with my patients. This is what makes my work even more rewarding. Yet sometimes such concentration has negative aspects.

During the creation of this book my enthusiasm was so great for the writing that I found myself feeling impatient during my time with my family. I wanted so much to return to my writing. When I recognized this problem, I reoriented myself. I told myself (self-statement) that while with my family there was no point in being impatient and that I should spend quality time with them as well as quality time writing. I practiced focusing on my family while with them and focusing on the book when writing. I felt better and more relaxed. I had controlled my thoughts, which in turn affected my feelings and my behavior.

As my real-life example illustrates, breaking the cycle of thought, behavior and emotion, is best achieved when the thoughts are altered. Here are some thoughts commonly associated with anger:

- "He did this purposely."
- "She did this to spite me."
- "He did this to make me look like a fool."
- "She disobeyed me and that is unacceptable."

These thoughts are based on faulty logic or reasoning that was probably learned in the past. Such thoughts are called "irrational." You need to recognize irrational thoughts that are associated with anger. Then you can change them.

:60 Second Exercise: Irrational Anger

List your irrational angry thoughts and then next to each one dispute it in writing. For example, an irrational thought might be: *I'm angry with my wife for not dropping off my dry cleaning.* The disputing thought could then be: *My wife didn't forget this to spite me. She may have had a hard day at work and just couldn't get to it.*

Irrational Thoughts

1) _____

2) _____

3) _____

4) _____

5) _____

Dispute Each One

1) _____

2) _____

3) _____

4) _____

5) _____

Many irrational thoughts are based on shoulds, oughts and musts. "He must have dinner on the table when I get home." This could be changed from a must to a preference. "I would prefer that he had dinner on the table, but it is not mandatory." Such thinking will lead to less anger.

In reality, in the area of relationships there are few shoulds, oughts or musts. People can do as they see fit regardless of what we think. It is really our preference that they—our significant others—do as we wish. By thinking in terms of should, ought and must, we invoke an idea of some outside authority involved in our being right, in what we want or expect and in another person being wrong for not doing what we want or not agreeing with us. Right and wrong does not apply to most relationship issues. Each individual has his or her own beliefs, perceptions and feelings. Later we will learn that in emotional conflicts in relationships, we need to spend time trying to understand the other person's point of view. Neither person is right or wrong. You see it one way. The other person sees it differently. Communication about these viewpoints is more constructive than arguments over who is right and wrong. Communication can lead to negotiation, which will help us work out differing ideas, viewpoints or feelings.

:60 Second Exercise: *Should, Ought* and *Must*

You may have many ideas that include the word *should, ought* or *must* in them. List your *should, ought* or *must* thoughts as self-statements. Then, change each thought to a preference.

Shoulds, Oughts, Musts	Preferences
1) _____	1) _____
2) _____	2) _____
3) _____	3) _____
4) _____	4) _____
5) _____	5) _____

:60 Second Thought for the Day

You are what you think... So think positive thoughts! Remember, thoughts are self-fulfilling prophecies.

Distraction from angry thoughts may be appropriate at times. When you are stewing about something that angers you, distract yourself. Distracting activities can include listening to music or talk radio, watching television or picking up a magazine or book. You may even choose to replace angry thoughts with pleasant memories or experiences. This often is not just a one time shifting of thoughts. If you find anger-related thoughts creeping back into your consciousness over and over, you need to refocus over and over.

:60 Second Exercise: Distractions

List distracting activities that work best for you so that you will readily know what to do to replace stewing and brewing over angry feelings.

1) _____

2) _____

3) _____

4) _____

5) _____

:60 Second Exercise: Memories and Experiences

List some pleasant memories or experiences to focus on instead of angry thoughts.

1) _____

2) _____

3) _____

4) _____

5) _____

Another useful distraction technique is called "thought stopping." The individual simply says or thinks "STOP!" when an angry thought intrudes. Sometimes a rubber band is worn on the wrist to be snapped as we say "STOP!" to ourselves.

Another technique borrows from relaxation training. We can have more control over our thoughts when we are calmer. Remember, strong emotions drive strong thoughts, which in turn drive strong emotions. By repeating to ourselves the words "calm" when we breathe in through the nose and "peace" when we breathe out through the mouth, we are relaxing and giving our minds something to focus on. This blocks out other emotionally disturbing thoughts.

:60 Seconds to Master Worry

What is worry? Worry is <u>sustained</u> fear. It is negative goal setting. When we set positive goals or expect the best in a situation, we typically experience good things. However, in negative goal setting, we think about what we *do not* want to happen. When we think negatively, we draw negatives into our life. The antidote to worry is purposeful action, which is also the opposite of worry. Worry causes us to remain locked in indecision, while purposeful action requires and encourages decision-making. Use the following formula to master your worries.

1. Define exactly what it is that you are worried about.
2. Write down your worries. Fifty percent of the time, you will find a solution to your problem once you write it down.
3. Determine what is the worst possible outcome. Is it the loss of a job? The collapse of a relationship? Write down the worst possible outcome.
4. Now write down the second worst possible outcome.
5. Then resolve to accept the worst and whatever happens. In most instances you will be able to handle the result.
6. Next, improve upon the worst case scenario: write down concrete steps to take to make sure it does not happen.

Do these positive things. Take purposeful action. Understand that worry is simply an unwillingness or perceived inability to face your fears. Once you have prepared for and expect to face the worst possible outcome, the stress you feel dissipates like air from a deflating balloon.

:60 Second Exercise: Master Your Worry

1) What is it that you are worried about?

_____

_____

_____

_____

2) Define exactly what it is that you are worried will happen.

_____

_____

_____

_____

3) What is the worst possible outcome?

_____

_____

_____

_____

4) What are the steps (purposeful action) necessary to make sure the worst does not happen?

_____

_____

_____

_____

5) What is the second worst thing that could happen?

_____

_____

_____

_____

6) What are the steps (purposeful action) necessary to make sure the second worst situation does not happen?

_____

_____

_____

_____

7) Resolve to expect the worst and accept what happens; enjoy knowing you have the strength to take a chance and your preparation will help you avoid the worst-case scenario. Write down your thoughts now that you have done this exercise. For example, you may write, *At least I tried. I faced my fear and survived. I got things off my chest.* Add your own comments below.

_____

_____

_____

_____

Distorted thinking is a negative, debilitating way of viewing the world and relationships. Among the types of distorted thinking are:

1. **Filtering:** Taking the negative details and magnifying them while filtering out all the positive aspects of a situation.

2. **Polarized Thinking:** Categorizing things as black or white, good or bad. You have to be perfect, or you're a failure. There is no middle ground.

3. **Overgeneralization:** Coming to a general conclusion based on a single incident or piece of evidence. If something bad happens once, you expect it to happen over and over.

4. **Mind Reading:** Without real knowledge, believing you know what people are feeling and why they act the way they do. In particular, defining how people are feeling toward you.

5. **Catastrophizing:** Expecting disaster. You notice or hear about a problem and start, "What ifs:" What if tragedy strikes? What if it happens to you?

6. **Personalization:** Thinking that everything people do or say is some kind of reaction to you. Comparing yourself to others, trying to determine who is smarter, better looking, etc.

7. **Control Fallacies:** Feeling externally controlled, seeing yourself as helpless, a victim of fate. The fallacy of internal control has you responsible for the pain and happiness of everyone around you.

8. **Fallacy of Fairness:** Feeling resentful because you think you know what is fair and other people will not agree with you.

9. **Blaming:** Holding other people responsible for your pain or blaming yourself for every problem or reversal.

10. **Shoulds:** Having a list of ironclad rules about how you and other people should act. People who break the rules anger you and you feel guilty if you violate the rules.

11. **Emotional Reasoning:** Believing that what you feel must be true automatically. If you feel stupid and boring, then you must be stupid and boring.

12. **Fallacy of Change:** Expecting that other people will change to suit you if you pressure or cajole them enough. You feel the need to change people, because your hopes for happiness seem to depend entirely on them.

13. **Global Labeling:** Generalizing and making one or two qualities into a negative global judgment.

14. **Being Right:** Being continually on trial to prove that your opinions and actions are correct. Being wrong is unthinkable and you will go to any length to demonstrate your rightness.

15. **Heaven's Reward Fallacy:** Expecting all your sacrifice and self-denial to pay off, as if some higher being is keeping score. You feel better when a reward does not come to others.

Styles of Distorted Thinking

Do you recognize any of the ways you use distorted thinking?

1. **Filtering**

This distortion is characterized by a sort of tunnel vision, looking at only one element of the situation to the exclusion of everything else. A single detail is picked out and the whole event or situation is colored by the detail. A draftsman who was uncomfortable with criticism was praised by his boss for the quality of his recent detailed drawings and asked if he couldn't get the next job out a little quicker. He went home depressed, having decided that his employer thought he was dawdling. He selected only one component of the conversation on which to respond. He didn't hear the praise because of his nagging fear of criticism.

Each person has his own particular tunnel to look through. Some are hypersensitive to anything suggesting loss or failure and blind to any indication of gain or success. For others, the slightest possibility of danger sticks out like a barb in a scene that is otherwise warm with contentment. Depressed people select elements suggesting loss from their environment, those prone to anxiety select danger and those who frequently feel angry select evidence of injustice.

The process of remembering can also be very selective. From your entire history and stock of experience, you may habitually remember only certain kinds of events. As a result, you may review your past and re-experience situations that characteristically leave you angry, anxious or depressed.

By the very process of filtering you magnify and "awfulize" your thoughts. When you pull negative things out of context, isolated from all the good experiences around you, you make them larger and more detrimental than they really are. The end result is that all your fears, losses and irritations become exaggerated in importance, because they fill your awareness to the exclusion of everything else. Keywords for this kind of filtering are "Terrible... Awful... Disgusting... Horrendous." A key phrase is, "I can't stand it."

2. Polarized Thinking

The hallmark of this distortion is an insistence on "all or nothing" choices. You tend to perceive everything at the extremes, with very little room for a middle ground. People and things are good or bad, wonderful or horrible. This creates a black and white world and, because you miss all the nuances of gray, your reactions to events swing from one emotional extreme to another. The greatest danger in polarized thinking is its impact on how you judge yourself. If you aren't perfect or brilliant, then you must be a failure or an imbecile. There is no room for mistakes or mediocrity. A charter bus driver told himself he was a real loser when he took the wrong freeway exit and had to drive several miles out of his way. One mistake and he thought of himself as incompetent and worthless. A single parent with three children was determined to be strong and "in charge." The moment she felt tired or slightly anxious, she began thinking of herself as weak, then grew disgusted with her "lack of strength" and criticized herself in conversations with friends.

3. Overgeneralization

In this distortion you make a broad, generalized conclusion based on a single incident or piece of evidence. One slipped stitch means "I'll never learn to sew." A rejection on the dance floor means "Nobody will ever want to dance with me." If you got sick on the train once, you will never take a train again. If you felt anxious the last time your husband took a business trip, you'll be a wreck every time he leaves town. One bad experience means that whenever you are in a similar situation, you will repeat the bad experience.

This distortion inevitably leads to a more and more restricted life. Overgeneralizations are often couched in the form of absolute statements, as if there were some immutable law that governs and limits your chance for happiness. You are overgeneralizing when you conclude with certainty that "Nobody loves me..." "I'll never be able to trust anyone again..." "I'll always be sad..." "I could never get a better job..." "No one would stay my friend if they really knew me." Your conclusion is based on one or two pieces of evidence and ignores everything you know about yourself to the contrary. Cue words that indicate you may be overgeneralizing are *all, every, none, never, always, everybody* and *nobody*.

4. Mind Reading

When you mind read you make snap judgments about others: "He is just acting that way, because he is jealous..." "She is with you for your money..." "He is afraid to show he cares." There is no evidence, but it just seems right. In most instances, mind readers make assumptions about how other people are feeling and what motivates them. For example, you may conclude, "He visited her three times last week, because he was...

(a)...in love."

(b)...angry at his old girlfriend and knew she would find out."

(c)...depressed and on the rebound."

(d)...afraid of being alone."

You can take your choice, but acting on any of these arbitrary conclusions may be disastrous.

As a mind reader, you also make assumptions about how people are reacting to things around them, particularly how they are reacting to you. "When he gets this close, he'll see how unattractive I am..." "She thinks I'm really immature..." "They're getting ready to fire me." These assumptions are usually untested. They come from intuition, hunches, vague misgivings or one or two past experiences. The evidence may be shaky, but the assumptions are believed to be rock solid truths.

Mind reading depends on a process called projection. You imagine that people feel the same way you do and react to things the same way you do. Therefore, you do not watch or listen closely enough to notice that they are actually different. If you get angry when someone is late, you imagine everyone acts that way. If you feel excruciatingly sensitive to rejection, you expect most people to feel the same. If you are very judgmental about particular habits and traits, you assume others share your beliefs. Mind readers jump to conclusions that are true for them without checking whether they are true for the other person.

5. Catastrophizing

Catastrophizing is seeking small events as disasters: a small leak in the sailboat means "It will surely sink." A contractor who gets underbid concludes "I'll never get another job." A headache suggests that brain cancer is looming. Catastrophic thoughts often start with the words "what if." Reading a newspaper article describing a tragedy or hearing gossip about some disaster happening to an acquaintance, you start wondering if it will happen to you. "What if I break my leg skiing?" "What if my car crashes?" "What if I get sick and have to go on disability?" "What if my son starts taking drugs?" The list is endless.

6. Personalization

Personalization is the tendency to relate everything around you to yourself. A somewhat depressed mother blames herself when she sees any sadness in her children. A recently married man thinks that every time his wife talks about tiredness she means she is tired of him. A man whose wife complains about rising prices hears the complaint as an attack on his ability as a provider.

A major aspect of personalization is the habit of continually comparing yourself to other people:

"He plays piano so much better than I do..."

"I'm not smart enough to go with this crowd..."

"She knows herself a lot better than I do..."

"He feels things so deeply while I'm dead inside..."

"I'm the slowest person in the office..."

"He's dumb (and I'm smart)..."

"I'm better looking..."

"They listen to her, but not to me."

The opportunities for comparison never end. The underlying assumption is that your worth is questionable. You are therefore continually forced to test your value as a person by measuring yourself against others. If you come out better, you have a moment of relief. If you come up short, you feel diminished. The basic thinking error in personalization is that you interpret each experience, each conversation, each look as a clue to your worth and value.

7. Control Fallacies

There are two ways which distort your sense of power and control. You can see yourself as helpless and externally controlled or as omnipotent and responsible for everyone around you.

Feeling externally controlled keeps you stuck. You do not believe you can really affect the basic shape of your life, let alone make any difference in the world. Everywhere you look you see evidence of human helplessness. Someone or something else is responsible for your pain, your loss and your failure. They did it to you. You find it difficult to strive for solutions, because you think they probably would not work anyway. An extreme example of this fallacy is the person who walks through skid row wearing three diamond rings and a five-hundred-dollar watch. He feels helpless and resentful when he gets mugged. He can't imagine how he had anything to do with it. He was the passive victim. The truth of the matter is we are constantly making decisions and every decision affects our lives.

The opposite of the fallacy of external control is the fallacy of omnipotent control. If you experience this distortion, you feel responsible for everything and everybody. You carry the world on your shoulders. Everyone at work depends on you. Your friends depend on you. You are responsible for the happiness of many people and any neglect on your part may leave them lonely, rejected, lost or frightened. You have to right all wrongs, fill every need and calm every hurt. And if you do not, you feel guilty. Omnipotence depends on three elements: a sensitivity to the needs of people around you, an exaggerated belief in your power to fill those needs and the expectation that you, and not they, are responsible for filling those needs.

8. **Fallacy of Fairness**

Fairness is a subjective assessment of how much of what one individual expected, needed or hoped for has been provided by another person. The trouble here is that two people seldom agree on what fairness is and there is no court to help them. When you conveniently define fairness so that each person gets locked into his or her own point of view, the result is a sense of living in a war zone and a feeling of ever-growing resentment.

The fallacy of fairness is expressed in conditions and assumptions: "If he loved me, he would do the dishes..." "If this was a real marriage, she would hike with me and learn to like it..." "If he cared at all, he would come home right after work..." "If they valued my work here, they would give me a promotion."

It is tempting to make assumptions about how things would change if people were only fair or really valued you. However, the other person may not see it that way and you end up causing yourself a lot of pain.

9. **Blaming**

Blaming often involves making someone else responsible for choices and decisions that are actually your own responsibility. There is great relief in having someone to blame. If you are suffering, someone must be responsible. You are lonely, hurt or frightened and someone provoked those feelings. A woman blamed her butcher for selling hamburger that was always full of fat. It was really her problem. She could have paid more for leaner meat or gone to a different butcher. In blame systems, somebody is always doing it to you and you have no responsibility to assert your needs, say no or go elsewhere for what you want.

Some people focus blame exclusively on themselves. They criticize themselves constantly for being incompetent, insensitive, stupid, too emotional, etc. They are always ready to be wrong. One woman felt she had spoiled her husband's entire evening when she caused a fifteen-minute delay in getting to a party. Later, when the party broke up early, she decided that she had bored everyone.

10. Shoulds

"Shoulds" make you operate from a list of inflexible rules about how you and other people should act. According to this thinking, the rules are right and cannot be disputed. Any deviation from such particular values or standards is bad. As a result, the person operating from this distortion is often in the position of judging and finding fault. People irritate him. They do not act "right" and they do not think "right." They have unacceptable traits, habits and opinions that make them hard to tolerate. They *should* know the rules and they *should* follow them. Kate, one woman, felt her husband *should* want to take her on Sunday drives. She felt a man who loved his wife *ought* to take her to the country and then go out to eat in a nice place. The fact that he did not want to go meant that he "only thought about himself." Cue words indicating the presence of this distortion are *should, ought* or *must*.

Not only are other people being judged, but the person who uses "shoulds" is also making himself suffer. Those who use the "should" distorted way of thinking feel compelled to do something or be a certain way, but never bother to ask objectively if it really makes sense.

:60 Second List: Common Yet Unreasonable "Shoulds"
- I should be the model of generosity, consideration, dignity, courage, unselfishness.
- I should be the perfect lover, friend, parent, teacher, student, spouse.
- I should be able to endure any hardship.
- I should be able to find a quick solution to every problem.

- I should never feel hurt; I should always be happy and serene.
- I should know, understand and foresee everything.
- I should always be spontaneous and at the same time I should always control my feelings.
- I should never feel certain emotions, such as anger or jealousy.
- I should love my children equally.
- I should never make mistakes.
- I should have consistent emotions—once I feel love I should always feel love.
- I should be totally self-reliant.
- I should assert myself and at the same time I should never hurt anybody else.
- I should never be tired or get sick.
- I should always be at peak efficiency.

11. Emotional Reasoning

At the root of this distortion is the belief that what you feel must be true. If you feel like a loser, then you must be a loser. If you feel guilty, then you must have done something wrong. If you feel ugly, then you must be ugly. If you feel angry, someone must have taken advantage of you.

All the negative things you feel about yourself and others must be true, because they feel true. The problem with emotional reasoning is that emotions by themselves have no validity. If a person has distorted thoughts and beliefs, her emotions will reflect those distortions. Always believing your emotions is like believing everything you see in print without checking sources or verifying the validity.

12. Fallacy of Change

The fallacy of change assumes that other people will change to suit you if you just pressure them enough. Your attention and energy become focused on others, because your hopes for happiness lie in getting them to meet your needs. Strategies for changing others include blaming, demanding, withholding and trading. The usual result is that the other person feels attacked or pushed around and does not change at all. The underlying assumption of this thinking style is that your happiness depends on the actions of others. In fact, your happiness depends on the many thousands of large and small decisions you make during your life. The only person you can really control or have much hope of changing is yourself.

13. Global Labeling

Global labeling generalizes one or two qualities into a global judgment. The label ignores all evidence to the contrary. Your view of the world becomes stereotyped and one-dimensional. For instance, you believe your supermarket stocks rotten food at rip-off prices. A person who refuses to give you a lift home is a total jerk. You assume a quiet guy is really a snob. Your boss is a gutless imbecile. Lawyers all are a bunch of money-hungry predators. While each of these labels may contain a grain of the truth, practicing global labeling prevents you from seeing the larger truth or the complexity of a particular situation or individual.

14. Being Right

The person using this distortion is usually on the defensive. He must continually prove that his viewpoint is correct, his assumptions about the world and all of his actions are correct. He is not interested in a differing opinion, only in defending his own. He never makes mistakes. His opinions rarely change, because he has difficulty hearing new information. If the facts do not fit what he believes, he ignores them.

Bob, an auto mechanic, got in the habit of stopping at a bar for three or four drinks on the way home. Frequently, he got home after seven o'clock and his wife never knew when to have dinner ready. When she confronted him, he got angry and said, "A man has a right to relax. You have it easy while I was pulling off cylinder heads all day." In his mind, Bob had to be right and could not comprehend his wife's viewpoint.

Having to be right makes a person very hard of hearing. It also makes that person lonely, because being right seems more important than an honest, caring relationship.

15. Heaven's Reward Fallacy

In this framework for viewing the world, the person using it always does the "right thing" in the hopes of receiving a reward. She sacrifices and slaves and imagines that she is collecting brownie points that she can cash in some day.

Alice, a housewife, cooked elaborate meals for her family and did endless baking and sewing. She drove her children to all their after school activities. The house was immaculate. She did this for years, always waiting for some kind of special reward or appreciation. It never came. She became increasingly angry, hostile and bitter. The problem was that while Alice was doing the "right thing," she was physically and emotionally bankrupting herself. She had become angry and reproachful and no one wanted to be around her.

:60 Second Exercise: Distorted Thinking

As you were reading through the distortions, you probably noticed some that you often use. Others you may have found you rarely if ever indulge in. Your high-frequency distortions are the ones you need to sensitize yourself to so that your inner alarm sounds whenever they come up. Before going on, read and familiarize yourself with them. List those you employ often and write down specific examples of when and how you use them.

1) _____

2) _____

3) _____

4) _____

5) _____

:60 Second Tips: Thinking and Anger

- Remember we can only think one thing at a time.
- Choose what you think.
- Control the things you think or say to yourself in your head.
- Focus your thoughts on the constructive.
- Break the cycle of feeling, thinking and acting on the level of your thoughts.
- Accept that due to learning, our thoughts can be irrational.
- Know that there are many categories of irrational thought.
- Learn to dispute irrational thoughts.
- Be aware of *should, ought* and *must* thinking. Think preferences instead.
- Master your worry.
- Be aware of your irrational and distorted thinking styles.
- Distract yourself from angry thoughts.
- Use thought stopping techniques and borrow from your relaxation skills when anger flares.

CHAPTER 11

Anger in the Workplace

*"Work joyfully and peacefully, knowing that right thoughts
and right efforts inevitably bring about right results."*
-James Allen

Workplace anger is a rising problem not only in America, but around the world. Add to the everyday stresses of modern business life the fear and fury about terrorism in our midsts after the attacks on the World Trade Center and the Pentagon and the possibility for further flare-ups by individuals pushed beyond their limits is considerable. In recent months, as security has tightened, eroding as it must some personal liberties, many people have become agitated and frustrated—a combustible mixture.

Yet I must point out that even before September 11, 2001, workplace rage was inflicting increasing damage. As anger in the workplace becomes a part of our daily lives, we must take steps to relieve that anger by changing our work habits, our work environment and/or our relationships with coworkers and bosses. First and foremost, however, we must learn positive anger management techniques so that if all else fails, we can still count on ourselves to squelch negative, destructive acting out.

Vicky's story will give you a sense of the damage such anger can cause. Vicky is a victim of workplace anger. She came to see me due to the severe distress she was experiencing after an incident with a supervisor. Vicky was a letter carrier for the United States Postal Service (USPS). Her supervisor had a history of workplace anger, threats and violence.

His story had spread among the local workers of the USPS, which served to contribute to the extreme fear Vicky experienced.

The supervisor had been dating a postal employee. When she announced that she wanted to break off the relationship, he began stalking her. This culminated in a telephone call to her at work at a local post office. The supervisor told her he was coming to her postal station with a shotgun. He intended to kill her and then himself. Calls were made to the police, the station was shut down and the workers and customers hid under counters and desks. Sure enough, he showed up with a shotgun. The police were waiting for him and arrested him. The supervisor was taken to a psychiatric facility for observation and treatment. The Postal Service terminated him. After a period of treatment, the supervisor sued the Postal Service and won back his job. He returned to work as a supervisor in the station where Vicky worked.

One day while delivering mail on her route, the supervisor came upon Vicky while she was in her mail truck. He apparently thought she was not wearing her seatbelt and ordered her out of the truck. Vicky said that his face was red, his eyes were bulging and that he was screaming. She was aware of his past history, however, and needless to say Vicky was reluctant to get out of the truck. In fact, she locked the doors. This enraged the supervisor further. Vicky drove away and headed for an apartment complex where she delivered mail and was known by the management and the security guards. The supervisor followed her. Vicky ran for the apartment complex management office. She told the manager what was happening and security was called. The supervisor was escorted off the premises by security even though he falsely claimed that he was a postal inspector.

When Vicky returned to her postal station she was called into the manager's office. The manager and supervisor were there. She was informed that she was being immediately fired for insubordination. She had failed to follow the supervisor's orders by not exiting the truck.

Vicky fell into a state of deep depression. She also showed symptoms of post-traumatic stress disorder such as flashbacks, nightmares, fear, anxiety, panic attacks, a need to isolate herself in her home, a sense of general numbness and a loss of her identity as a strong, resourceful, independent individual who had worked to support her two children as a single mother.

Vicky has fought to recover ever since. Despite many setbacks and a sense of hopelessness and helplessness, she has won many victories. She never took matters into her own hands, but used the system to fight back. After a year and a half, Vicky won her job back through binding arbitration. She received lost pay, but could not recoup lost overtime which many postal employees rely upon to make ends meet. Soon after this Vicky won an appeal of her worker's compensation claim. She was the one of the first people in the history of federal employment to receive worker's compensation benefits for a purely psychological work injury. Vicky also sued the Postal Service and received a $105,000 settlement. All of these financial victories have not compensated Vicky for what she lost. She continues to suffer from depression and symptoms of post-traumatic stress disorder. She has lost her sense of well-being and her identity as a strong, independent individual. She says that the job, benefits and money will never make up for the damage done. To this day she is only able to work part-time on an inside job where she feels somewhat protected. By the way, the supervisor was fired again, but, after again suing the Postal Service, he won back his job, only to accost *another* female employee. When you wonder why the cost of stamps keeps going up, be aware that the Postal Service has paid out at least $355,000 in settlements for damages caused by the uncontrolled anger of one supervisor. That does not include the costs of grievances, arbitrations, hearings, legal fees, lost time and payment of lost wages and benefits.

The costs of workplace anger are many. Not only does it cost organizations money, but lives have been lost or damaged irreparably. Government statistics suggest that an average of twenty workers are murdered and 18,000 are assaulted while at work each week. Between July 1992 and July 1993 for example, 2.2 million full-time workers were attacked on the job, 6.3 million were threatened with violence and 16.1 million were harassed at work. These figures include assaults on employees by members of the public as well as worker on worker anger and violence.

As a result, the government and many employers have established workplace violence policies. Primary among these is a zero tolerance for violence at work. Threat Assessment Teams have been established and include representatives from human resources, employee assistance programs, security, unions, the workers, management and legal departments.

When violence or the threat of violence occurs among coworkers, firing the perpetrator has been noted not to be the most appropriate way to reduce the risk for additional or future violence. Employers realize there is a considerable advantage to retaining some control over the perpetrator and requiring and/or providing counseling or other care.

If you inappropriately act out on your anger in the workplace, realize that help is available. Seek intervention through human resources or the employee assistance program. This will help protect your job and will be invaluable in your private life as well.

Many on-the-job situations can cause anger. It will help you recognize and understand your angry feelings if you can pinpoint the reasons why anger occurs in the workplace. Some of the reasons may be:

· Experiencing conflict with supervisors or coworkers.
· Feeling overwhelmed by excessive or difficult work assignments.
· Having difficulty meeting deadlines.
· Perceiving a lack of support from superiors.
· Feeling powerless.

Add the reasons why *you* experience anger in your workplace.

1) _____

2) _____

3) _____

4) _____

Contrary to popular belief, most perpetrators of threats or violence in the workplace are not severely mentally disabled or ill. Research shows that such people are no more likely to commit crimes against others than the entire population. In other words, the people who are committing violent acts are generally classified as normal individuals. It is the people who are frustrated, thwarted, annoyed or threatened who behave aggressively in the workplace. This includes average, everyday people who are in bad situations and cannot handle their emotions, primarily anger, in a constructive way. This may even include you.

To prevent workplace violence, the following guidelines have been developed for organizations to follow:

- Create a supportive work environment in which violence is not tolerated.
- Develop policies which foster and encourage respect among managers and staff.
- Train supervisors to recognize signs of a troubled employee.
- Provide personal counseling for workers.
- Establish procedures for handling grievances.
- Train managers and employees to resolve conflicts in a peaceful manner.
- Provide training in human relations issues concentrating on communication styles, assertiveness training, conflict-resolution, reflective-listening techniques and instruction in the causes of violence in small and large groups.

In these guidelines we can see many of the positive coping skills you have learned in the preceding chapters of this book. Use them along with formal procedures for resolving conflict where you work.

To help identify people before they act out on anger at work, profiles have been compiled of those who have been violent in the workplace. These profiles include:

- History of violence
    - criminal acts
    - domestic violence
    - verbal abuse
    - anti-social behavior
- Romantic obsession
- Chemical dependence on alcohol or drugs which leads to decreased impulse control
- Depression (One in seven depressed people will commit an act of violence against themselves or others.)
- Pathological blaming (Individuals who accept no responsibility for their actions.)
- Impaired neurological functioning (This includes those who were hyperactive as children, those who have had brain injuries and those who have had abnormal EEG's. These people tend to be less capable of inhibiting themselves.)
- Demonstrated irritation with family, peers or coworkers

- Interest or obsession with weapons
- Personality disorders (Personality patterns become inflexible, impaired and unhealthy; some of these people can be very rigid and cannot be reasoned with.)

Use these as signs or signals for yourself. If you meet one or two criteria, are feeling angry at work and have begun thinking about acting out on anger or are making self-statements about doing harm, seek help. Go to your employee assistance program or seek private counseling to head off acting out in a way that will be destructive to others and yourself.

Supervisors and managers must be trained to look for:

- Alcohol abuse
- Drug abuse
- Impaired judgment
- Emotional difficulties
- Financial problems
- Legal problems
- Strained family relations
- Occupational failures
- Threats

Again, use these as *your* early warning signs and take responsible action.

When a supervisor has documented that there is a decline in job performance, which is not job related, and that the employee has previously shown the capability of performing his or her job, the Employee Assistance Program is contacted. The employee is given help. Many supervisors are now documenting the following signs of risk:

- Absenteeism
- Personal Appearance, Attitude and Behavior
    - Personal appearance becomes sloppy
    - Wide mood swings
    - Smell of alcohol or frequent use of breath spray
    - Repeated accidents
- Interpersonal Relations
    - Complaints from co-workers
    - Complaints from clients
    - Overreaction to criticism or suggestions

- Shifting of work responsibilities to others
- Avoiding associates
· On the Job Absenteeism
  - Absent from post
  - Long lunches
  - Preoccupation
· Job Efficiency
  - Erratic or deteriorating productivity
  - Missed deadlines
  - Failure to follow instructions
  - Errors in judgment

:60 Second Exercise: Workplace Threats

Document workplace problems you are experiencing below. Write down any of the early warning signs of workplace threats or violence that may apply to you now.

_____

_____

_____

_____

_____

_____

_____

_____

_____

_____

_____

_____

The primary cause for workplace anger has been identified as stress. The body's response to any demand on it for adaptation is called stress. A stressor may be acute or chronic. Stress can be both good and bad. Examples of good workplace stress are deadlines and competition. Often, we need a certain amount of stress to function. It motivates us to perform; without it people can stagnate. The level of anxiety caused by a good stressor is usually in the low to moderate range. Levels of high anxiety are okay for short periods of time. If the levels of high anxiety last for an extended period, however, then the stressor is bad and the person becomes overwhelmed or impaired in his or her functioning. Inability to escape from or adapt to stress can cause clinical depression, chemical dependence or other personal breakdowns.

Some of the ways you can alleviate job-related stress are:

- Communicate honestly with supervisors and colleagues; express feelings and emotions.
- Schedule downtime; don't do work on your lunch or coffee break—take a walk instead.
- Break large projects down into smaller, more manageable segments.
- Delegate responsibility whenever possible.
- Set aside time each day to really relax; try to banish thoughts of work during this time.
- Keep up-to-date with your work skills.
- Say "no" when necessary.
- Participate in some form of daily physical exercise.

Ed is a perfect example of work-induced stress leading to anger. He came to me after working twenty-five years for a package shipping company. Ed was normally an easygoing guy who was well liked by peers. He came in with depression and panic attacks which made him want to flee from work. At the age of forty-five he never had to seek psychological help before. It seemed that Ed had been having an ongoing conflict with his supervisor. Ed drove a truck and delivered packages. Drivers must deliver all the packages on their route each day. The number of packages depends on the type of route. Ed had been having to use overtime to complete his deliveries. His supervisor was warning him and writing him up for using too much overtime. Ed knew from the previous driver on his route that management had increased the size of his territory just before Ed took over. From his experience Ed knew that his route needed to be re-evaluated—the territory was too big. There is a procedure for requesting this. Ed made the request and was wrongfully turned down. Meanwhile, he was on the verge of being suspended for using too much overtime. The next step would be termination. Ed needed only five more years before he could retire with a nice pension. This would be lost if he was fired. Ed filed grievances with the help of his union, but these take some time until they are heard. They are also heard by the same managers who are involved in the problem. In this no-win situation, Ed was becoming more and more frustrated and angry. He felt he had no outlet for his frustration or way to address his problems. Ed was not the type to get aggressive, so instead he became depressed. He turned the anger against himself. He also had panic attacks. These were a release of built up anger that he could not express. The energy had to come out somehow.

I placed Ed on leave to get him away from the extreme and previously inescapable stress. We worked on his depression and on rebuilding his coping skills. In the meantime, he sought help from the union vice president. Utilizing the system to address his problems with management, Ed won a grievance and his route was re-evaluated. Sure enough, the size of his territory was reduced. This was all he had been looking for. Upon returning to work, Ed found that he was still being mildly harassed by his supervisor. Before going out on deliveries, drivers spend a couple of hours in the warehouse organizing their trucks for the route. Ed's supervisor would stand right behind him for long periods. Using the anger management skills I taught him, Ed took matters into his own hands. He requested a meeting with his supervisor so they could calmly talk things out. Ed left the meeting he had initiated feeling pretty satisfied that they had cleared the air. He was also proud that he stood up for himself without inciting a loud, ugly, angry scene. Ed and his supervisor came to an understanding that day and began working on a new, healthy relationship. Now, they use humor to cut through any tension that arises and they've learned to talk things out before small irritations blossom into huge problems.

:60 Second Exercise: Frustration at Work

Write down all of the techniques you can use to address work-related frustration. These can include skills you utilize on-the-job, like relaxation techniques, or things you do on your own time at home, like engaging in physical exercise.

_____

_____

_____

_____

_____

_____

_____

:60 Second Exercise: Stress Reduction

Write down examples of how you can use your skills to constructively address stressors at work. For example, these can include sitting down and talking things out (using communication), documenting (journaling), filing grievances (being assertive) or walking away (taking a Time Out).

_____

_____

_____

_____

_____

_____

_____

One of my clients, Ron, worked for a medium-sized commercial printing firm. He would come to see me periodically when stress began building up at work. One time, Ron had stood up for a coworker who was being unfairly harassed by a supervisor. When Ron stood up for his coworker, he became the focus of the supervisor's harassment. This built up over a few days to the point where Ron wanted to hit the supervisor. He knew better than to do it. Ron knew he would lose his job. He immediately said he was going home sick and came to see me. Ron needed time to cool down. He knew his rights granted by his union contract and used this knowledge to fight back against the supervisor and management. Ron knew he had done nothing wrong. A series of grievance meetings erased all of the reprimands leveled by the supervisor. All pay lost for suspensions was returned also through the grievance procedure.

Another time Ron was being blamed for the breakdown of an expensive collating machine. As much as he tried to explain that a repairman had been unable to properly fix it long before Ron attempted to use the machine, management would not accept his refusal to take responsibility. Ron felt he was being set up to take the fall and felt his anger building to a point of wanting to act on it. Again, before he got himself in to serious trouble, Ron announced he was going home sick. Ron is to be commended for recognizing his anger, pulling back from acting out on it destructively, seeking help, utilizing his anger management techniques and using the grievance system in his workplace to protect himself and assert his rights without resorting to violence.

:60 Second Tips: Workplace Anger

- Workplace threats and violence should no longer be tolerated.
- Organizations should establish relevant policies, response teams, profiles, prevention and help programs.
- Recognize the presence of risk signs in yourself.
- Seek help if you have been thinking of acting out in anger on the job.
- Utilize your new coping skills at work.
- Use the existing systems at your place of employment to address conflicts and assert your rights.
- Use the legal system to settle major grievances. Seek legal advice and assistance if all else has failed at work.

CHAPTER 12

Catastrophic Stress/Catastrophic Anger

*"The earth is always shifting, the light is always changing... The moment
we cease to hold each other, the sea engulfs us and the light goes out."*
-James Baldwin

I learned of the horrific terrorist attacks of September 11, 2001 when my father called. I picked up the telephone and he said, "Something terrible happened this morning. Four planes were hijacked. Two of the airliners crashed into the World Trade Center towers and they toppled. Another plane crashed into the Pentagon. The fourth plane crashed somewhere in Pennsylvania." Immediately I flashed back to the day President Kennedy was assassinated. I was seven years old, in the third grade at P.S. 105 in the Bronx, New York. The voice of the principal, Mr. Stark, came over the loudspeaker in the classroom. He told us what had happened and that school was being closed. There was a strange atmosphere as I began to walk the four blocks home from school with my friends. Back in those days we all walked to and from school. It was a more innocent time when parents did not have to worry about their children being snatched or assaulted. It was the middle of a weekday and yet the streets were filled with adults and children alike. It just did not seem right or real. Then I saw my Dad walking toward me on the sidewalk. I was surprised and glad to see him. I felt suddenly safer and more secure. He had come home early from work, as had many other fathers. Everything in the country had stopped.

I retain snippets of personal memories of the days following the assassination of President Kennedy. I remember the feeling of sadness now forever connected to the sight of John Kennedy, Jr. saluting his father's casket. I remember my father stopping short in his tracks as he tried to figure out bullet trajectories with the aid of an illustration published in the *New York Times*. As he shifted from an intellectual approach to an emotional one, Dad began shouting something about Lee Harvey Oswald, Kennedy's assassin, having the skin peeled off his back.

I remember those days as vividly as we will remember where we were and what we were doing on September 11, 2001. As I reflect on my reactions as a child and as an adult, I realize that they are similar. There are alternating periods of disbelief, sadness and anger. It will take a long time, if ever, to arrive at resolution, the end point and the purpose of the grieving process. We will grieve over the event, because once again we have experienced loss and we will now live with even more horrendous worries. As Joel Garreau of the *Washington Post* wrote on September 12, 2001: "Heart-rending, first person descriptions of horror mingled with level-headed analysis and warnings against precipitous action while cries for vengeance flowed..."

Internet sites served as virtual support groups. A chat room called "Lean on Me" tried to provide consolation through prayer and words of condolence for people worried about their loved ones, but most of the entries were filled with anger, profanity and stereotyping of Pakistanis, Muslims, Zionists, Mexicans and others. Many of the comments expressed rage and disbelief. "An eye for an eye," wrote one contributor to the chat room discussion.

Although there was generalized anger toward the perpetrators of the attacks, for some the anger became generalized toward others thought to be members of the same culture or religion as the terrorists.

In the weeks following the attacks, many talked about taking out terrorists or bombing those who have supported terrorists. We have all been shifting from intellectually dealing with the attacks to reacting purely based on our emotions and back again. This is a normal process. When we talk about taking aggressive action, we feel a relief of our built-up outrage. We are venting our angry feelings. This is helpful, as long as we express such feelings in words, but never in actions. Unfortunately, some of us have crossed a line and taken destructive actions against people because of their ethnic background or religious faith. This diminishes us all.

The anger we feel in response to catastrophic events is acceptable, understandable and normal. Once again, what we do with it or how we express it is the key. All of our anger management techniques should be applied to help us express and channel our personal and national anger in constructive, healthy ways.

On the national level we can use our government's actions as a positive model for coping. We did not see from our leaders a leap or rush into action. Anger was set aside and a more thoughtful, patient approach was taken to ensure our future safety. Assertion, communication and negotiation were utilized. Assertion, for example, was seen in the British Prime Minister Tony Blair's statement to the Taliban that they either turn over Osama bin Laden or lose power. Communication was used in our President's address to the joint session of Congress. Negotiation was implemented in the diplomatic initiatives taken to form a coalition of nations against terrorism. We, too, in our private reactions to the events of September 11, can use assertion, communication and negotiation to good effect.

In the first week after the attack my patients spoke of nothing else. In the face of such traumatic events, we all need to talk. We need to feel heard and understood. This is therapeutic and cathartic. Talk with your loved ones. Listen to your family and friends. It is especially important to express your feelings with children. This shows them that it is okay to feel sad or afraid or angry and how to express these emotions constructively. Encourage them to talk to you or to draw their feelings in pictures. One six-year-old I know spontaneously drew a picture of an airplane, a tall building and people falling out of the building. The images and feelings are there. Do not be afraid of encouraging children's expressions. It is okay to let your children see you cry and to encourage them to express their emotions by showing and saying that it is okay to cry. This will only help. Do not rush to deny or negate feelings. Express first, listen next and then reassure.

Check in with others periodically. Check in with yourself, too. Tune in to feelings. Accept your own. Accept those of others. Encourage the airing of feelings by yourself and others. When there is no one around to listen or talk with, write your feelings in a journal.

One of my early reactions to the events of September 11 was an intense need to do something, to help. Being a member of the Army Reserve and a psychologist, I made a telephone call and offered my immediate availability. I offered assistance in debriefing and counseling the injured, survivors, family members and rescue workers. I knew by helping someone else I would help myself as well. Channel your anger into this kind of positive action. Take some time to brainstorm on your own and with family and friends to come up with ways you can help, whether you donate blood, contribute to a charity, etc. Offer children opportunities to help, too.

Following the attacks on the World Trade Center and the Pentagon, we saw a tremendous coming together of people to volunteer and to help. This is an intuitive and powerful coping mechanism. Thousands of public safety personnel flocked to New York City to help with the rescue. Tens of thousands gave blood, prayed, donated money and participated in rallies or religious services. These are all important coping mechanisms.

As time goes by after this or any catastrophe, remember these important examples of coping. Keep looking for opportunities to contribute, to come together with others, to express and share emotions, to help those in need because of the trauma. You will have the dual benefits of helping others and helping yourself. Remember, it is okay to help yourself.

Knowing what you are feeling will help you deal with your anger through positive actions—physical activities like taking a walk, going for a run and cleaning house. If you want to hit something, try a tennis ball, baseball or racquetball or the stress reducing techniques of meditation or deep breathing we have learned. Do not take your anger out on those around you through the negative means of physical or verbal abuse. Displacing anger unto others will not bring relief, but merely compounds your feelings of anxiety.

Never before have so many people been able to watch death over and over again on television. In the face of such nationally viewed and experienced trauma and catastrophic stressors, we all need help. Many may need professional counseling. There is a list of resources at the end of this chapter.

The trauma of terrorism isn't only physical, it is psychological. Even those who only watched the events on television may experience great stress since the brain records memories from viewing such horror. These are difficult images to handle and yet many will never get them out of their minds. However, reacting with rage and violent aggression should be of particular concern to everyone. After September 11, a lot of angry retorts were heard: "We should bomb them out of existence," "We have to get revenge," "Better dead than alive."

If you or someone close shows increasing anger after several weeks, is angry much of the time or is acting out inappropriately, let the person talk out their feelings. Expressing oneself verbally is one good way of getting control. If you or they worsen or withdraw, get professional help.

This does not mean you're crazy, but that your ability to cope is impaired because the scope of these events is overwhelming. Addressing post-traumatic issues will help you move from the anger you feel about your country and its citizens becoming victims to taking positive steps to express emotions constructively.

Another good way to express your feelings constructively is to document them in a journal. This is especially helpful for those who have difficulty verbalizing their emotions or who just aren't up to talking to others about their feelings yet. An exercise in journaling, related specifically to the tragic events of September 11 and their aftermath, can be found on the following page.

:60 Second Exercise: Journaling
Catastrophic Stress/Catastrophic Anger Journal

Copy and use this page to journal what you are feeling in response to the catastrophic stress of September 11, 2001. Though some time has passed, reflect back to that infamous day. What were your feelings on that day and in the days and weeks that followed? What are your feelings today? How have they changed? What will you do with your feelings now? Write your answers to the preceding questions on the blank lines below. When you are finished, put the page and your feelings aside. Distract yourself from your feelings for a while. We need to pace ourselves, to give ourselves breaks. You may wish to do this at several intervals. Strike a balance between feeling, thinking and constructive action.

_____

_____

_____

_____

_____

_____

_____

_____

_____

_____

_____

_____

_____

_____

:60 Second Exercise: Constructive Acts to Handle
Stress and Anger Caused by Catastrophic Events

In the wake of traumatic and tragic events, people often ask, "What can I do to help?" It feels good to help others and, in so doing, we help ourselves by releasing our strong emotions in constructive, positive ways. If we don't have positive outlets through which we can release these negative emotions, stress and anger can build up. On this page brainstorm some ideas about the healthy, positive actions you can take to channel your angry feelings. Write a commitment to take at least one positive action each week.

1) _____

_____

_____

2) _____

_____

_____

3) _____

_____

_____

I commit myself to: _____

_____

_____

:60 Second Exercise: Terror-Based Irrational Thoughts

Fear and anger can be a highly dangerous combination. They may lead to violent acts against oneself or others. On this page list any irrational angry thoughts you have about catastrophic stressors induced by the terroristic acts of September 11. Then dispute each one. For example:

Thought: *I'm going to go out armed with a loaded gun every day and keep it by my bed at night.*

Disputation: *A loaded gun improperly kept could be dangerous for my children and might cause me to take precipitous action.*

Thought: *Never trust anyone of Islamic faith.*

Disputation: *I'm overgeneralizing. There are many members of the Islamic faith who died in the World Trade Center or are as hurt by the terrorist attacks of September 11, 2001 as I am.*

Thought: *There is a mosque in our town. I should get my friends and we'll go bust some windows.*

Disputation: *I feel anger, but I am not going to commit violent acts against others. Then the terrorists will have won.*

Thought: _____

_____

Disputation: _____

_____

Thought: _____

_____

Disputation: _____

_____

Thought: _____

_____

Disputation: _____

_____

Thought: _____

_____

Disputation: _____

_____

The American Psychological Association Web Site (www.apa.org) offers the following resources:

For the Public
·   Resources for Coping with Traumatic Events
·   Coping with Terrorism
·   Reactions and Guidelines for Children Following Trauma/Disaster
·   Managing Traumatic Stress: Tips for Recovering from Disasters and Other Traumatic Events
·   Coping with the Aftermath of Disaster
·   Warning Signs of Trauma-Related Stress
·   How to Find a Therapist

For Rescue Workers
·   Disaster Manual from the National Center for Post-traumatic Stress Disorder
·   Information for Rescue and Response Workers
·   Secondary Stress and the Professional Helper
·   Compassion Fatigue and Secondary/Vicarious Traumatization

Advice for Parents

- Talking with Children about Traumatic Events
- Helping Children Who Have Witnessed Violence
- What Makes Kids Care
- Advice to Help Your Kids Maintain Loving, Compassionate Qualities in the Face of Violence

---

:60 Second Tips: Handling Catastrophic Events Stressors

- Accept that we will always remember where we were and what we were doing at the time of a catastrophe.
- Know that it is normal to alternate from disbelief to sadness to anger and over again after a national or personal trauma.
- Recognize our anger is normal and understandable.
- Remember statements of revenge are a way to vent our built up outrage.
- Know expressing our collective anger in words is okay. Acting on it is not.
- Express your anger in words, in writing, in pictures.
- Give children help and encouragement in expressing their feelings.
- Check in with yourself and others periodically.
- Channel anger and stress into helping others.
- Keep looking for opportunities to contribute, to come together with others, to express and share emotions.
- Find resources on the American Psychological Association Web Site (www.apa.org) and other crisis intervention organizations' web sites such as the Red Cross (www.redcross.org).

PART III

REINFORCING POSITIVE CHANGES

*"You have not converted a man because
you have silenced him."*
-John Morley

CHAPTER 13

Do You Feel Lucky Today?:
Assertiveness Skills

"He that always gives way to others will end in having no principles of his own."

-Aesop

By being aware of triggers and cues and utilizing Time Outs, relaxation techniques and self-control of thoughts, your actions will stabilize and become effective to introduce other techniques which go beyond direct anger management. We can now work on heading off destructive anger in the first place. We will focus in Part III on assertiveness training, communication skills training, negotiation training, the role of substance use and abuse and the necessity of seeking outside help.

In the film *Dirty Harry*, Inspector Harry Callahan points a gun at a would-be robber and says, "You've got to ask yourself one question: 'Do I feel lucky today?' Well, do ya, punk?" Callahan was not an individual one would classify as merely assertive. He was very aggressive and so were his methods of apprehending criminals and questioning suspects in the movie.

Assertiveness Continuum

Aggressive   **Assertive**   **Passive**

◄───►

Being assertive, a positive trait, needs to be understood as a midpoint on a continuum. At the extreme far ends of the continuum are two negative traits, being aggressive and being passive. Neither of these is constructive nor healthy. Aggression hurts others, the aggressor and any witnesses (such as children who grow up listening to Mommy and Daddy argue or watching their physical abusiveness). Depending on the circumstances and whether an individual is over or under-controlled in his or her hostility, remorse and guilt may follow aggressive behavior. This leads to low self-esteem and sets the stage for the next incident of abuse.

Passivity is equally harmful, especially to individuals who engage in such behavior. It is also harmful to others who may not be protected from aggressive people because of caretakers' passivity (such as many abused children whose non-abusive parents fail to take action to protect them). Passive individuals internalize anger, seething inside, instead of dealing constructively with emotions. This may lead to medical problems (e.g., ulcers) or psychological problems (e.g., depression, anxiety, panic attacks). Many passive individuals also feel shame and beat themselves up emotionally as they dwell on what they wished they had said or done. It is not that passive people do not act out on their anger. On the contrary, they quite often do, however their acting out can be seen not in yelling or overt aggressive behavior, but in their inaction. In other words, out of accumulated anger, spite and grudge-holding, passive people purposely withhold what others ask of them. For example, with no explanation they may cut off writing or calling old friends who have angered or slighted them.

It must be remembered that people do not engage in their aggressive or passive behavior because they are bad or flawed. This is learned behavior and there are usually very good reasons for it. For example, many people who have suffered abuse become passive to avoid more abuse and because their self-images have been so damaged.

Diana was in her middle forties when she first came to see me. I had been recommended to her by the Employee Assistance Program at her workplace. Diana was a detective. Her complaint was that she was experiencing anxiety and was concerned because her family doctor had recommended a minor tranquilizer. Diana would not say much more than this. Police officers learn not to trust others, especially people who work within the mental health units of their own agencies. Cops call police department psychiatrists the "rubber gun squad," because there are times when law enforcement officers are experiencing such severe difficulties that the mental health unit will recommend removal of their firearms and temporary assignments to desk jobs during treatment.

Diana was not pressured to speak about her anxiety at our first few meetings for fear that it might scare her away from therapy. Instead, she was educated about anxiety and taught relaxation exercises. Biofeedback was used to help her strengthen the relaxation response. What she learned about anxiety was that it is often driven by unexpressed anger. It comes out in the form of some sort of energy or agitation labeled by the individual as anxiety and nerves. In Diana's case, she revealed that she had experienced several panic attacks. These were first interpreted by her to be heart attacks (racing heartbeat, hyperventilation, faintness) leading her to several emergency room visits. Each time she was prescribed tranquilizers and sent home.

After about the sixth session, Diana seemed less interested in being hooked up to the biofeedback equipment. She wanted to talk and suddenly a lot came pouring out. Diana, who specialized in handling domestic violence cases, was being emotionally and physically abused by her husband. Diana literally felt handcuffed or paralyzed, because her husband threatened to turn her into internal affairs for being a drunk and for abusing him. Later we found out that Diana's husband was abusive, because he had been emotionally, physically and sexually abused by his father.

Diana had been attracted to her future husband while a college student, because he was so needy and clung to her for help. Diana had been brought up in a very religious and moral family. She was a caretaker and so chose professions and relationships where she was called upon to help others. Diana spent twenty years with her husband. They had two children together. This was another bond which kept her in the relationship. During their early years together, her husband revealed himself to be increasingly unstable. He abused substances and made several suicide gestures. He also threatened to kill Diana and the children. On the assertiveness continuum, Diana's husband would be way out on the aggressive end. Diana would be equally extreme in her passivity. She was afraid to express herself, because her husband would yell curses and put-downs at her in front of the children. She clammed up and withdrew in exasperation in the face of his intense, violent anger. During counseling,

Diana was given permission to express her feelings and take care of her own needs.

Eventually Diana and her husband divorced and she was awarded custody of the children. About one year later, Diana met someone and was engaged to be married. But her divorce had been ugly and the period after was even uglier. Diana was still being harassed by her ex-husband who had not formed any new relationships and would not let go of her. He was enraged at her for leaving him and committing to another man.

At first, Diana continued to remain passive and internalized her newly realized anger. After a while, however, she moved to the other extreme and began acting out aggressively. Over time and due to the stress of her own self-defeating outbursts of anger and frustration, Diana learned to assert herself more constructively. She became able to simply say no to her ex-husband without having to apologize or explain herself and, in the other extreme, without yelling. The calmer she was, the less he could get to her. She was no longer rewarding her ex-husband with the negative attention he provoked. Diana had found the positive, healthy mid-point on the assertiveness continuum.

Like Diana, you too can learn assertiveness. This brings us back to our ultimate goal: Being able to express angry feelings calmly and in words, without attacking or putting down others. If you feel heard, you are more likely to get your feelings attended to and have your needs met. The other person has no reason to be defensive or attack back. You will communicate calmly and effectively and come across as stable and credible. You do not need to exert power or control over others, because you are empowered. There is no power struggle, because you side-step it. You will show others that it is not control that's important, but communicating effectively. One's ego or self-esteem is not at stake, which in reality is irrelevant in most encounters with other people anyway. For, you cannot get your self-esteem from others. It must come from within yourself, from what you think about yourself and what you say about yourself in your mind, the latter being your self-statements.

Since low self-esteem can cause anger problems, it needs to be worked on. In the next exercise, list some of the negative things you think about yourself or say about yourself privately or in your mind.

Then, next to each one write down the opposite, a positive statement. Since many of our negative self-statements are irrational, it is important that we replace them with positive self-statements. Our faulty or irrational negative self-statements often involve should, ought and must thinking. Read through your negative self-statements and look for the words should, ought or must. Change those words to preferences. Instead of thinking, *I should be more patient with my ex-wife* or *I should make dinner more often*, change these self-statements to, *It would have been better if I were more patient with my ex-wife* or *It would be nice if I made dinner more often*. This leaves you room for self-tolerance rather than self-condemnation, for change rather than the sense that you have permanently failed and can do nothing to redeem yourself. If you feel you need to work on some before you can really believe in the positive statements, the list can focus your efforts on what you need to do to feel better about yourself. In time, you will be able to believe in the positive self-statements.

:60 Second Exercise: Self-Esteem

To improve self-esteem, list some of the negative things you think about yourself or say about yourself in your mind. Next to each one write down the opposite, a positive statement about yourself.

Negative Self-statements	**Positive Self-statements**
1) _____	1) _____
_____	_____
_____	_____
_____	_____
_____	_____
2) _____	2) _____
_____	_____

_____   _____

_____   _____

_____   _____

3) _____   3) _____

_____   _____

_____   _____

_____   _____

_____   _____

4) _____   4) _____

_____   _____

_____   _____

_____   _____

:60 Second Exercise: Getting in Touch with Oneself

In order to assess ourselves, we need to know what we are feeling. Many people have difficulty getting in touch with their emotions. As part of the process of learning to recognize feelings, a list of emotions follows. Next to each one try to fill in some of the physiological sensations you have felt that you think go along with the different emotions.

For example, next to "angry" you might put "muscle tension" or "rapid heart beat." For "furious" you might say "heart pounding," "hot," or "face flushed." This exercise will help you tune in to your body's physical responses, which are signals to help you tune into your emotions.

Emotion	Physical Sensations
Irritated	_____
Annoyed	_____
Frustrated	_____
Pissed Off	_____
Enraged	_____
Furious	_____
Explosive	_____
Nervous	_____
Anxious	_____
Panicky	_____
Frightened	_____
Terrified	_____
Blue	_____
Sad	_____
Despairing	_____
Amused	_____
Happy	_____
Joyous	_____

Difficulty getting in touch with one's emotions is an underlying problem in positive assertiveness. If a person does not know what he feels, he cannot express his emotions or wants. He then builds up resentment, thinking irrationally that others "should" read his mind or know what he feels or wants. He may even think others are purposely with-holding their understanding or depriving him of his wants.

Feelings are a part of our human nature. We all have them. Feelings, therefore, are a common ground for relating and communicating with other people. When I am aware of my feelings and yours, I am in a position to respond more appropriately and thus, communicate more effectively.

Why focus on feelings?

We all "hide" to some extent. In "hiding" we can be false, dishonest, inconsistent and misleading. We deceive ourselves and others. Repression is one common way of "hiding." We all have some feelings we do not like. They are uncomfortable, unpleasant and unwelcome, so we try to avoid them. One way to avoid feelings (temporarily) is to suppress them: to shove them aside, tuck them out of sight, disregard, ignore or conceal them. By suppressing them we can pretend we do not have them. On the other hand, we all have some feelings we do like. They are comfortable, pleasant and welcome feelings. So we often pretend we have them.

:60 Second Exercise: Feelings

What feelings do you like and sometimes pretend to have?

What feelings do you dislike and sometimes pretend not to have?

_____   _____

_____   _____

_____   _____

_____   _____

_____   _____

_____   _____

_____   _____

_____   _____

In addition to the fact that we all like and dislike some feelings, there are approvals and disapprovals placed on certain feelings. Some feelings are okay, others are not. We are told (by ourselves and others) not to have "bad" feelings and to try to always have "good" feelings. When we do experience negative emotions or thoughts, we feel guilty. We often label both our feelings and ourselves as "bad." We experience remorse and loss of self-esteem; we feel unworthy; we despise and reject ourselves. We expect the same reactions from others. This is an uncomfortable situation, so we pretend we do not have those "bad" feelings. This is when hiding, or suppression, comes in.

On the other hand, we receive from others and give ourselves approval to have "good" feelings. When we have these good feelings, we feel better about ourselves; we respect ourselves and we feel righteous. For this reason, many people pretend to always have them.

:60 Second Exercise: "Bad" and "Good" Feelings

List some examples:

__What are your "bad" feelings?__	__What are your "good" feelings?__
_____	_____
_____	_____
_____	_____
_____	_____
_____	_____
_____	_____
_____	_____
_____	_____

A necessary condition for discovering feelings and developing empathy for others' feelings, is to regard them as simply there and to accept them as present in ourselves and others, whether we like them or not and without labeling them "good" or "bad." One of my patients had been physically, sexually and emotionally abused as a child. Deborah had also been threatened by her father with severe consequences if she ever told or expressed to others any feelings about what he was doing to her. For Deborah, her feelings became "bad," even dangerous. The only thing left for Deborah was to split herself off from the abuse and her emotions. Deborah carried this into her adult life, long after her father died. Once she overcame her fear, however, a flood of emotions came back to Deborah. She asked me, "What do I do with these emotions?" I responded, "Have them." Once she gave herself permission to have them, we spent a long time dealing with the emotions she felt.

Another reason for focusing on feelings is the fact that ordinarily we do not do so. We discuss ideas, intellectualize, analyze problems, express opinions, exchange fantasies and memories, play golf, play poker and have some physical contact with each other. For the most part, we ignore or shove aside our feelings. We not only do not share feelings, we simply do not know how. We build defenses to protect and hide our feelings. Feelings are out of bounds for most of us and there are defenses and barriers between us. We cannot really know each other when large and significant parts of us are hidden from view. We do not know what to expect of each other. We mistrust each other. We remain constantly on guard, defensive, wary, cautious and distant. We live as strangers, even as enemies to each other.

Feelings are here and now and need to be recognized. We are inter-acting with each other constantly on an emotional level with a common pool of immediate data with which to deal. We are all actually partici-pating in a shared experience.

:60 Second Feeling Discernment

1. Feelings are a basic unit of human experience.
2. A small number of feelings underlie much of the human experience.
3. All feelings are okay.
4. Feelings will continue to recycle until we *allow* ourselves to experience them deeply.
5. Feelings will recycle until we *accept* ourselves for experiencing them.
6. The direct expression of basic feelings can result in clear, meaningful communication.

7. Directly stated feelings and wants often are the key to solving problems among individuals.
8. Feelings that have not been accepted will recycle in the form of unproductive thoughts and behaviors.
9. The "way out" is always through experiencing the feelings, even if they bring pain and conflict.
10. What we resist controls us.

:60 Second Chart: Thoughts and Feelings

Emotion or Experience	Related Thoughts
Sadness or depression	You have thoughts of loss: a romantic rejection, the death of a loved one, the loss of a job or the failure to achieve an important personal goal.
Guilt or shame	You believe that you have hurt someone or that you have failed to live up to your own standards. Guilt results from self-condemnation, whereas shame involves the fear that you'll lose face when others find out about what you did or didn't do.
Anger, annoyance, irritation or resentment	You feel that someone is treating you unfairly or trying to take advantage of you.
Frustration	You feel that life falls short of your expectations. You insist that things should be different. It might be your own performance ("I shouldn't have made that mistake"), what someone else does ("He should have been on time!") or an event ("Why does the traffic always slow down when I'm in a hurry?").

Anxiety, worry, fear, nervousness or panic	You believe you are in danger, because you think something bad is about to happen. "What if the plane crashes?" "What if my mind goes blank when I give my speech in front of all those people?" "What if this chest pain is the start of a heart attack?"
Inferiority or inadequacy	You compare yourself to others and conclude that you are not as good as they are, because you are not as talented, attractive, charming, successful, intelligent. "She has really got what it takes. She is so cute. All the men are chasing her. I'm just average. There is nothing very special about me."
Loneliness	You tell yourself that you are bound to feel unhappy, because you are alone and you are not getting enough love and attention from others.
Hopelessness or discouragement	You feel convinced that your problems will go on forever and that things will never improve. "I'll never get over this depression."

:60 Second Feelings Descriptions

Anger	Fear	Guilt
· Displeased	· Afraid	· Remorseful
· Indignant	· Frightened	· Feeling of having
· Exasperated	· Timid	done wrong
· Irritated	· Alarmed	
· Annoyed	· Uneasy	Lonely
· Frustrated	· Anxious	· Isolated
· Dejected		· Low spirits

Shame
· Embarrassed
· Humiliated
· Chagrined
· Foolish
· Ashamed
· Inadequate
· Insufficient
· Lacking
· Incomplete
· Crazy
· Worthless
· Dumb

Happy
· Pleasure
· Contented
· Glad
· Joyous

Sad
· Sorrowful
· Melancholic
· Mournful
· Hurt
· Pained

Resentment
· Unresolved anger

:60 Second Exercise: Defensive Feelings

Fill in the blank spaces with the feelings you think are most appropriate. Some have already been filled in to guide you in this exercise.

Defenses	How people may see us	Possible hidden feelings
Explaining		
Justifying	Self-pitying	
Intellectualizing	Superior	
Rationalizing	Arrogant, Intolerant	
Minimizing	Controlled	
Theorizing	Manipulative	
Analyzing		
Switching		
Generalizing		
Glaring		Angry
Disagreeing	Stubborn	Sad
Sarcastic	Defiant	Afraid
Threatening	Hostile	Shame
Attacking	Angry	Hurt, Guilty
Agreeing		Lonely
Flattering	People Pleaser	Inadequate
Joking	Nice Guy	
Smiling	Wishy-washy	

Apologetic	Phony	_____
Charming	_____	
Minimizing	Aloof	_____
Evading	Indifferent	_____
Switching/	Rejecting	_____
Shifting		
Silent	Sullen	_____
Withdrawing	Suspicious	Dejected, remorseful
Running Away	_____	Shame, humiliated
Projecting		_____
Critical	Angry	_____
Moralizing	Resentful	_____
Judgmental	Martyr, Intolerant	Insecure

When two people in an unsatisfying relationship are asked how they feel, they often answer with something like "I feel as though he lectures me" or "I feel like she is not listening to me." These are not feeling statements. As we learned earlier, there are four basic feelings: Mad, Scared, Sad and Glad. Emotions, of course, vary greatly depending on how strongly one is feeling, but they all can still be classified as belonging in one of the four basic categories. There is a difference between "I feel *thinking*" statements versus "I feel *emotion*" statements. The examples above can be rephrased as "I feel <u>mad</u> that he lectures me. I would <u>like</u> to have conversations" or "I feel <u>mad</u> that she is not listening to me. I would <u>like</u> to have a chance to talk."

:60 Second Exercise: Assertiveness Tool

The next exercise has to do with learning to put your verbal expressions of emotion into a new, positive, constructive format. Think about something that makes you angry. Now, write it out in two sentences using the format in below.

<u>Assertion:</u>

I feel angry that _____

_____

I would like to _____

_____

Such statements are much less likely to be perceived by others as critical or attacking and so are less likely to be responded to defensively or with a counterattack. If you use this kind of descriptive communicating, you are more likely to receive understanding and a commitment from others to try harder to meet your needs. The communication is more constructive and effective, so it will be reinforced. In the long run, communicating with statements that describe your feelings and how you would prefer to be treated will gain results. Remember Dennis? Had he not changed he might have continued to get his way, but he also was highly likely to lose his wife, daily contact with his children, his home and his money. Once he began using this format of communication, he found greater satisfaction in his personal relationships as he learned to be less autocratic.

Now, practice putting several of your familiar anger statements into this new format:

I feel angry that _____

_____

I would like to _____

_____

I feel angry that _____

_____

I would like to _____

_____

I feel angry that _____

_____

I would like to _____

_____

Read the statements to yourself. Now, say them aloud. Next, say them aloud to someone else. Keep writing and speaking these statements until using this format becomes second nature. Whenever you feel angry, state your feelings using this new format. When you do so, reward yourself. Treat yourself to a pleasant activity or something you enjoy. Ask for feedback from others around you. "How did you feel when I expressed my anger that way?" They are more likely to respond positively when you use this format. Remember, though, that you have no control over how another person will act or respond. Let go of the expectation that he "must" appreciate it or she "ought" to respond positively. These are your preferences, but not statements of fact. Stay focused on the only person you can ultimately control: YOU. Do not give up even if the other individual does not appreciate it. You can appreciate yourself for your changes.

Another part of assertiveness is saying "NO." Many people have a hard time saying no or turning someone down. They feel compelled to do things for others they often do not want to do. Afterwards they feel resentment or fail to do what they promised and then they feel they must offer lengthy explanations for why they can't do what another wants. Sometimes they even find it easier to make up stories than to say no. Some people even structure their lives differently to avoid saying no. I have known people who chose to sell their trucks rather than deal with saying no to others who constantly asked them to help haul large items or move furniture. I've also known people who've moved to get away from family members who asked for favors all the time.

Rather than turn your life upside-down or take drastic measures to avoid people, learn to say no. Practice saying a simple and pleasant "No" when someone asks you to do something you do not want to do. Tell the person, "I'm sorry, but I can't." Offer no explanation. Notice how many successful business people or people who are self-employed make simple NO statements when asked for extras or price breaks, for example.

Assertiveness involves being able to say no, directly asking for what you want and expressing your feelings in the "I feel... I would like...." format. It does not involve attacking others nor suppressing your feelings.

:60 Second Exercise: Saying No

Make a list of some people you know. Imagine saying no to them or asking something of them. Is it easy or difficult to say no? Rank these people in order from one (easiest to say no to) to ten (hardest to say no to) by writing their names on the appropriate line. You may put more than one name on each line.

Easiest

1) _____

2) _____

3) _____

4) _____

5) _____

6) _____

7) _____

8) _____

9) _____

10) _____

Hardest

This week practice assertiveness by starting with the person you have labeled easiest. Ask that person for something that is clear or concrete and do so directly using "I" statements. In week two try this formula with the next person on your list and so on. As you progress it will get easier. The discomfort will dissipate as you become desensitized to it.

You will probably get all sorts of unexpected reactions. In some cases you may find that what you expected or thought would happen was different than what actually happened. In other cases the person's reaction may not surprise you at all.

In addition to asking for your wants and needs to be met, practice saying no without having to explain your response. If you have trouble getting started with the people on your list, tell a trusted friend or loved one about the exercise and its purpose. Ask that person to help you through role playing. The support person should pretend to be someone on your list and then ask you for a favor. Do your best to imagine you are really interacting with the person on your list, not the role player. In response to the request, give a firm but polite, "No." Ask the support person to give you positive reactions to increase your positive expectations.

When I was in graduate school, the professor who was teaching about assertiveness gave each of us an assignment. Mine was to walk up to a total stranger and ask for a quarter to make a call. I was nervous and had irrational thoughts about being rebuffed and rejected. However, the very first person I approached did not hesitate and said, "Sure." It was much easier than I had imagined it in my mind. The lesson to be learned here is that a person will react however she wants, not how you expect or hope her to. Remember, you can only control yourself, your words and your actions. Don't let your expectations of others sabotage your efforts to become assertive and to control your anger.

:60 Second Tips: Being Assertive

♦ Assertiveness is the midpoint on a continuum from aggression to passivity.

♦ Aggression and passivity are destructive to others and ourselves and they are unhealthy reactions.

♦ Aggressive and passive behavior is learned and can be unlearned.

♦ Assertive behavior can be learned.

♦ Being assertive involves expressing oneself calmly in words and not attacking or putting down the other person.

♦ Sidestep unneeded power struggles.

♦ Assertion requires self-esteem. You need to value yourself before you can stand up for yourself in a positive, constructive way.

♦ Replace negative thoughts about yourself with positive ones.

♦ Change *shoulds, oughts* and *musts* to preferences in the way you think about yourself and others.

♦ Tune into physical sensations to tune into your emotions. You need to know what you are feeling before you can express it.

♦ Examine how you hide your feelings.

♦ Express your feelings in "I feel...*emotion*" statements, not "I feel...*thinking*" statements.

♦ Use the format "I feel angry that... I would like..."

♦ Work on saying a simple "No" when you do not want to do something another person asks.

CHAPTER 14

Read My Lips: Communication Techniques

"It is better to debate a question without settling it than to settle a question without debating it."

-Jeseph Joubert

Communication theory tells us that there are many opportunities for signals or messages to be lost or distorted. The transmitter may change the message or add noise to the message. As it travels through the air, the signal or message can further be distorted.

Transmitter → Air → Receiver

The receiver changes the message as well. Do you remember the game of "telephone"? One person starts by whispering a message to another person. That person passes along the message to the next person and others continue passing it from person to person in a group and wait to see how much the message has changed by the time it reaches the last person in the chain. Almost always the message is garbled if not completely mangled. The same thing often happens when people communicate directly with each other.

Face-to-face communication starts with a person having a thought. The person then tries to find the best words to express that thought. This is the first filtering of the intended message. The person who receives the verbal message then takes it in and translates it according to his own understanding, vocabulary and experiences with language. This is a second filtering of the initial intended message. This receiving person formulates a response in his mind and then tries to find words to express it. There are many opportunities for miscommunication with all of this translating and filtering going on. We each have our own understanding of words. What a word signifies to one person may be completely different than another person's understanding. Add in that we often do not listen carefully; that we frequently are thinking of what *we* want to say while we are waiting for the other person's lips to stop moving. Factor in non-verbal communication such as facial expressions and body language. Then add in an emotionally charged issue and different perceptions of the same events ("You never wash the dishes." "I wash them three times a week. Boy, I wish the doctor could come home with us, so he can see how you lie."). The end result is miscommunication. Effective communication is not easy and like all other valuable skills, it takes time and effort to be improved.

:60 Second Types of Dysfunctional Communication

1. **Explaining too soon:** "Look, don't be hurt because I missed dinner. I just had to get away by myself." (Hidden message: *You have no right to feel that way.*)

2. **Reassuring before responding to feeling:** "You do not have to be hurt (scared, angry, etc.)." (Hidden message: *You shouldn't feel that way.*)

3. **Condescending:** "Tell me about it. I want to <u>help</u> you." (Hidden message: *I'm so sensitive and you are so weak.*)

4. **Blackmailing:** "You are giving me a headache (heart attack, depression)." (Hidden message: *I'm so sensitive and you are a brute who will stop at nothing to hurt me physically or mentally.*)

5. **Responding too soon:** Stating "I'm sorry, I did not mean it, I know just how you feel..." before the other has a chance to express his feelings fully. (Hidden message: *I do not want to hear what you have to say.*)

6. **Interrupting:** "You are hostile to me, because I remind you of your mother." (Hidden message: *I do not care how you feel about me, you cannot move me.*)

7. **Punishing:** "Oh, yeah? Well, let me tell you what you did!" (Not-so-hidden message: *I'll get you, you dirty rat! You'll be sorry you picked on me.*)

8. **Pretending to be stupid:** "Sorry, I do not understand what you are talking about." (Hidden message: *...and I do not want to, so why don't you give up?*)

9. **Passing the buck:** "That's your problem." (Hidden message*: I do not care how you feel and I can't be bothered to address your complaints.*)

10. **Changing the subject by replying to the content, instead of the emotion:** i.e., getting into an intellectual discussion to avoid responding to the other's feelings. "That's interesting. I've often noticed that women tend to have that attitude toward men. Why do you suppose that is?" (Hidden message: *As an individual person, you are unimportant. Do not take yourself so seriously.*)

11. **Playing lawyer:** "When did I say that? I never said those words." (Hidden message: *You made a mistake in this minor detail. That proves you have no right to your feelings.*)

12. **Turning the whole thing into a joke with a witty remark:** "You're just a loveable, dopey duck." (Hidden message: *You are not worth taking seriously.*)

13. **Scolding:** "That's very rude." (Hidden message: *You are a vulgar child beneath my cultured notice. I cannot take your feelings seriously. You are worthless."*)

14. **Being bored or absent-minded:** "Sorry, I did not hear you. My mind wandered." (Hidden message: *Your feelings are unimportant. You are not worth my important time.*)

A common problem, especially in communication among couples, is that each one tends to debate about who is right and who is wrong. I point out to couples in counseling that right and wrong are often meaningless and unimportant. I tell couples I am not a judge and will not listen to their debate and make a final pronouncement on who is correct and who is incorrect. Instead, I redirect them to the importance of listening to and understanding each other's feelings and perceptions.

Feelings color perceptions. That is why witnesses to the same event often describe that event back in many differing ways. I remember an episode of the television series *Thirty Something*. The entire episode was devoted to replaying each of the main characters' memory of the same cocktail party. The individual memories were completely different. Each person colored the events to reflect best on himself or herself. Since feelings are not rational and can color perceptions, I point out that it is impossible and unimportant to establish who is the right one and who is the wrong one.

Another common problem in communication is that we tend to argue about two different things at the same time. Many times, if I let a couple go on without interrupting them and having them refocus, they will argue back and forth about two clearly different issues. When couples engage in arguments in counseling sessions, these are called enactments. They give the counselor the chance to see just what a couple's communication is like. A good couples' counselor will not let these go on for too long, because anger builds to the point where the session becomes useless. Someone usually ends up walking out.

An example of a couple that argued about different issues at the same time is Mack and Ivy. Mack stood up in the middle of a session and said to Ivy, "You are spoiled. You never grew up. Your parents overprotected you. I can't believe you do not even bother to balance the checkbook." Ivy responded, "You are a control freak. You think you are an expert on everything. I'm tired of your lectures and your know-it-all attitude. I do not bother to balance the checkbook, because I know you will think I did it wrong." I knew I had to interrupt an exchange that was spiraling out of control. "Let us ignore the acting out of anger via all the criticisms and put-downs for now," I said. This couple could go on endlessly in this tennis match of dueling issues. Mack had an issue with Ivy's lack of knowledge of finances, money management and investing and general laxness in her approach to something that was obviously pretty important to him. Ivy had an issue with Mack's controlling ways and his habit of lecturing her. They had never resolved these issues because of their poor communication skills. With all the anger and put-downs, neither would hear the other. Neither felt understood and so the duel would continue with each trying to make his or her point over and over again. By stopping the argument midstream and refocusing, we were able to make progress.

If you should ever find yourself needing couples counseling, question the counselor about his style. A good couples' counselor is an active one who takes control of the sessions and doesn't allow them to turn into arguing matches. The counselor should be empathetic to the views and feelings of each party. When I intervene, I usually do so on the level of pointing out vicious cycles that both parties contribute to and how they each can act differently. For example, "John, I notice that you tend to be the disciplinarian with the kids and sometimes you are tough on them. Wendy, you feel the need to step in and stand up for the kids, because they are your biological children. You and John end up being angry with each other and the kids slide out of another jam. There is no consistency; the kids know they do not have to listen, because there are never any consequences. John, you seem to be overcompensating for what you see as Wendy's laxness and are tough with the children even though they are not your biological children. Wendy, you seem to be overcompensating for what you see as John's being too hard on them and also, perhaps, because you feel guilty about the divorce from their father. I suggest that you, Wendy, need to become more active as the discipliner, and that you, John, become more of a friend to the kids for now. You can consult with Wendy, but Wendy is the implementer of the discipline. This way you can have a united front for the kids and discipline will be followed through and therefore more effective. You two will be acting as a team and not letting the kids drive a wedge between you."

If I can accurately reflect an understanding of a person's feeling, he or she will often move on to a deeper level. Feelings usually reside on different levels. Underneath angry feelings is often the feeling of pain or of being hurt. For many people, it is safer to express anger than pain. To express hurt requires us to make ourselves vulnerable. If you let someone know he has hurt you, he might hurt you further. Or he may understand your feeling and offer reassurance or comfort. An example is: "It hurt me that you turned on the television when I told you I was having a bad week." It would hurt more if he said, "Well who wants to hear it?" Yet it can be good to take the risk, because you might alternatively hear, "I'm sorry. Let's talk about it now." Effective communication means taking a risk on one person's part and effort on the other's. Being able to say "I'm sorry" is so essential yet so hard to do. If you want to express anger, use this as a cue to look deeper in yourself. Underlying the anger is probably hurt. If you are hearing anger from your partner or a loved one, sometimes you need to wade through the anger and offer comfort, rather than reacting defensively and getting angry back. As with Mack and Ivy, it is important to slow down, eliminate the verbal aggression and take turns discussing issues. I call this "tabling." One person tables his issue while the other addresses hers. After this is worked through, the other person gets to address his issue.

Another couple, Howard and Ellen, who constantly argued about their views on various topics, benefited from the explanation of the uselessness of the debate over who is right and who is wrong. They also benefited from the awareness of the need to take turns discussing one issue at a time. The couple took this awareness and modified their own communication behavior and became much more satisfied in their relationship. The reader can draw from this discussion some ideas about how to approach general communication differently. When a couple, like Mack and Ivy, are having more severe problems, there are skills to be learned and exercises to be practiced.

:60 Second Exercise: Holding the Floor

This technique brings communication under control and stops two people from talking or shouting louder than the other. It forces them to do more listening. I tell the couple to sit down in two chairs facing each other. There are to be no distractions. The television is turned off, the phone ringers are turned off, the answering machine is on, the kids are in bed, the in-laws are at their own homes, etc. The couple should take something soft like a pillow to pass back and forth. Ashtrays and other hard objects are discouraged since we would not want anyone hurling them or either person to get hurt. The person who has the pillow gets to talk. Couples need a concrete symbol of who holds the floor to overcome old habits of talking over each other, cutting each other off and not listening but thinking of what he or she wants to say. Explain the floor exercise to your partner. Use it to stop arguments. Practice for one hour, two times a week. He talks until he is done. He is done when he gives up the pillow. The pillow is not taken. It remains under the control of the person who has the floor until that person is ready to give it up. Then the other person holds the pillow until done and so forth. If you do not have the pillow, you do not talk or interrupt. You listen. Couples are told to practice this for one hour, two times a week. It injects some fun into the effort of working on communication and it produces a change. A more complicated tool and exercise is "Paraphrasing." Couples are instructed to practice this skill at home and also to use it when a controversial topic is being discussed. This could prevent the need for a Time Out. It can also be used to keep communication under control after a Time Out.

Paraphrasing takes sufficient concentration and effort that, if adhered to, will guarantee an absence of an argument. It slows communication down to one thought or sentence at a time. Before a person can respond with her single thought, not a paragraph, she must successfully paraphrase in her own words what she thought she heard her partner saying. She then seeks feedback. It forces close listening and clarification of misunderstandings as they occur. The communication is highly controlled and therefore much safer than arguing.

Many couples eventually incorporate these techniques into their normal conversation. I know they have made progress when I hear them saying, "So what I hear you saying is that..." When this happens the communication is going very well. Good communication skills greatly reduce the acting out of anger.

:60 Second Exercise: Paraphrasing

Person **A**:	Makes a statement expressing one idea, thought or feeling. Keep it to one sentence.
Person **B**:	Paraphrase. Say back in your own words what you heard **A** say and wait for **A** to give you feedback.
Person **A**:	Give feedback to **B** on the paraphrase of your statement. Did she hear you correctly or not? "That's right, that's what I was saying," or "Not quite."
Person **B**:	If you get it wrong, try again. Sometimes **A** may have to express the original point again to make it clear to

B. Person **B** must again try to accurately paraphrase what she heard **A** say before the exercise can go on. Once **A** says that your paraphrase was correct, that you demonstrated you understood what was said to you, then **B** gets a chance.

Person **A**: Gives feedback that the paraphrase was accurate.

Person **B**: Now, it is your chance to respond to **A**'s original statement. You can respond now with a statement expressing one idea, thought or feeling. Keep it to one sentence.

Person **A**: You must paraphrase what you heard **B** say.

Person **B**. Give feedback on the paraphrase.

Person **A**: If correct, it becomes your turn again. Respond to **B**'s statement with one sentence expressing your thought.

And so on.

You cannot ask questions while paraphrasing. Stay on track. Do not get impatient and break away from the paraphrasing format. This can lead back to problem communication. By staying with the paraphrasing technique, you will follow one issue to completion. I have often seen how this will lead to understanding when I walk a couple through the exercise in my office. It can also lead to a couple agreeing to disagree. When this happens, there are other techniques to learn which will be explained in the next chapter.

:60 Second Practice: Paraphrasing

Person **A**: Makes a statement expressing one thought.

Person **B**: Paraphrase **A**'s statement.

Person **A**: Give feedback on the paraphrase.

Person **B**: If correct, make a statement expressing one thought in response to **A**'s original statement.

Person **A**: Paraphrase **B**'s response.

Person **B**: Give feedback.

Person **A**: Make a statement.

And so on.

:60 Second Example #1: Paraphrasing Exercise

Person **A**:	"It is very humid outside today."
Person **B**:	"So you are saying the air is heavy out today."
Person **A**:	"No, that's not what I really meant. I meant the air is very thick."
Person **B**:	"Okay. So you are saying the air is dense, like it's hard to breathe."
Person **A**:	"I did not say it's hard to breathe, just that the air is dense."
Person **B**:	"You are saying it is humid and the air is dense."
Person **A**:	"Yes! Exactly! Your turn."
Person **B**:	"I agree that the air is thick today and I am having trouble breathing."
Person **A**:	"So you agree that the air is thick and it is making your breathing difficult."
Person **B**:	"That's it. You got it."
Person **A**:	"Since you are having trouble breathing and I find the humidity uncomfortable, let's go inside our nice air conditioned house."
Person **B**:	"So since we both are uncomfortable but in different ways, you are saying we should go inside."
Person **A**:	"That is exactly what I meant."
Person **B**:	"Well, I could not agree more."
Person **A**:	"You are saying you strongly agree."
Person **B**:	"Right."

A & B walk into the house hand in hand, smiling lovingly at one another.

I usually suggest use of paraphrasing on a mildly controversial topic during practice rather than a topic that acts as a real "hot button" issue between the two people. If you discuss something like the weather, as I have done in the previous example, the conversation is relatively short and few opportunities for arguing arise. Practice once a week from thirty to sixty minutes. Eventually, you will be familiar enough with this method of communication that you can use it to address some core conflicts as I have done in the following example.

:60 Second Example #2: Paraphrasing Exercise

Person **A**:   "I feel angry."

Person **B**:   "You are feeling angry."

Person **A**:   "Right."

Person **B**:   "Well, just the way you said right, your tone of voice is making me feel attacked and angry."

Person **A**:   "You are feeling attacked and angry, because I snapped at you; I was short with you in how I said 'right.'"

Person **B**:   "That is correct."

Person **A**:   "I'm sorry. I'll just express my feeling that I am angry, because it just seems to me that I do all the work when we have dinner."

Person **B**:   "You're angry since you feel you do all the work preparing dinner."

Person **A**:   "No. That's not all of it."

Person **B**:   "Oh. You're angry since you feel you do all the work at dinnertime."

Person **A**:   "That's it. That's what I'm feeling."

Person **B**:   "We can divide up the work."

Person **A**:   "You are saying we can divide up the work."

Person **B**:   "Yes."

Person **A**:   "I'll do everything one night and you do it the next."

Person **B**:   "You want to alternate doing everything for dinner night by night."

Person **A**:   "You heard that right."

Person **B**:   "I have a different idea. I propose that you prepare the meal and I will do the cleanup every night."

Person **A**:   "So you are saying we should divide it up differently. I do the cooking and you clean up."

Person **B**:   "Exactly!"

Person **A**:   "Well, I want to do the cleanup. You do the cooking."

Person **B**:   "You are saying you only want to do the cleanup."

Person **A**:   "That is right."

Person **B**:	"We have reached an impasse. We both want to do the cleanup and not the cooking."
Person **A**:	"You are saying we are deadlocked, because we both want to clean up and nobody wants to cook."
Person **B**:	"Yes."
Person **A**:	"Let's try to find a compromise."
Person **B**:	"You think we should compromise."
Person **A**:	"Right."
Person **B**:	"Let's switch off. I'll cook and you clean up one week. I'll clean up and you cook the next."
Person **A**:	"We'll alternate the cooking and cleaning up weekly."
Person **B**:	"Exactly."
Person **A**:	"Sounds good to me."
Person **B**:	"You are comfortable with that idea."
Person **A**:	"Yes."
Person **B**:	"Good, so it's agreed then."

People tend to lose track of their arguments, because they do what is called "kitchen sinking." They bring everything into the discussion but the kitchen sink. They get off the original issue and introduce other unrelated pet peeves and concerns. Paraphrasing keeps the discussion on one track, allowing the two people to resolve one conflict at a time without stirring up explosive anger.

:60 Second Exercise: Relationship Improvement #1

If you are having relationship problems, go out on a date with your partner. Upon first meeting, there is seldom anything as important as the new relationship. After a time the novelty wears off and the couple feels safe in their commitment to each other. Less effort goes into the relationship and more into everything else. Once children come along, they become the priority, followed by earning money, purchasing a home, taking care of older relatives, etc. The relationship is often taken for granted and is given little or no effort. Many people think that satisfaction should just happen, as it did when they first met. They should not have to work at their relationship. The truth is everything takes effort, including a relationship. Many couples literally spend almost no time together as a couple. Free time is devoted to family activities. Socializing may only occur with other couples. Inevitably the day comes when the men sit together in the front seat and the women together in the back. Did you ever see a couple do this during the first six months of their relationship? You can't keep them apart that long. Besides, they're usually too caught up in each other to pay attention to their friends.

I tell couples to think back to their courting days. They are to recreate some of those early dates. This needs to be done at least once a week. If money is an issue, there are always beaches or parks to walk in. If they can't leave home because of a lack of funds for a baby-sitter, they are instructed to have different quality time together. For example, one night after the children are asleep, unplug the telephone, turn off the television and spend some quality time together. This can mean playing a game, lighting some candles and snuggling on the couch, turning on soft music and dancing, etc. It is a shared responsibility. Each partner takes turns planning and arranging the date.

:60 Second Exercise: Relationship Improvement #2

Another exercise for those in relationships is for you to list three things you think your partner needs to change to improve the relationship. More importantly, you also list three things you need to change to improve the relationship. Your partner may work on the lists also, but this is his or her choice. Ultimately, you only have control over what you do. By focusing on the changes you need to make, you are putting your energy into what you really have control over. Do not wait for your partner to make the first move. It takes a risk or a leap of faith to initiate change. The hope is that your effort will be noticed, appreciated and reciprocated. It may take time to rebuild trust and rekindle positive feelings.

:60 Second List: Relationship Improvement

Blank lists for this exercise can be found on the following two pages. The first two sections of the list are for you to complete. If your partner is amenable, have him or her fill in the second two sections separately.

Three Things I Would Like
My Partner to Do to Make the Relationship Better:

1) _____

_____

_____

2) _____

_____

_____

3) _____

_____

_____

Three Things I Need to Do to Make the Relationship Better:

1) _____

_____

_____

2) _____

_____

_____

3) _____

_____

_____

For Your Partner (optional but even better).
Three Things I Would Like
My Partner to Do to Make the Relationship Better:

1) _____

_____

_____

2) _____

_____

_____

3) _____

_____

_____

Three Things I Need to Do to Make the Relationship Better:

1) _____

_____

_____

2) _____

_____

_____

3) _____

_____

_____

When done, sit down and read the lists. If you both have done them, read to each other. Make a commitment to work on your part. By recognizing your partner's needs, you are helping to rebuild the relationship. By exchanging them, you both are. Let your partner know that you will be putting effort into the things you can do to make the relationship better. Paste your list to your bathroom mirror or some other location that will require you to see it everyday.

:60 Second Axioms on Listening

"I know that you believe you understand
what you think I said,
But I'm not sure you realize that
what you heard
is not what I meant."

We Communicate
not by what we are,
but by what listeners understand.
We Communicate
not by what we intend to say,
but by what listeners see, hear,
and are willing to accept.
We Communicate
not by what we say,
but by what listeners hear.

:60 Second Tips: Communication

♦ Realize that original messages may be lost or distorted at many points in communication.

♦ Stop debating about who is right and who is wrong.

♦ Listen to feelings and perceptions.

♦ Address one issue at a time.

♦ Know that many people express anger rather than hurt (it is easier to do).

♦ Use anger as a cue to look deeper at what you are feeling. Risk expressing deeper feelings.

♦ Wade through another person's anger to provide comfort and to make it safe for them to express deeper feelings.

♦ Use and practice the Holding the Floor exercise.

♦ Use and practice the Paraphrasing technique.

♦ Avoid "kitchen sinking."

♦ Share in planning weekly dates.

♦ List three things you can do to make your relationship better.

♦ Post your list in a place that forces you to look at it everyday.

CHAPTER 15

Signing on the Dotted Line:
Negotiating and Contracting

"Any change, even a change for the better,
is always accompanied by drawbacks and discomforts."
-Arnold Bennett

Invariably couples say to me, "Okay, we understand we disagree and why. So what do you do when all this communication leads to an impasse?" Good communication skills usually lead to clarification of feelings and perceptions. This leads to increased mutual understanding and empathy which results in decreased conflict. There are times, however, when it will bring a basic difference or impasse into clearer focus. This is good. How many times have you forgotten what started an argument? Once a difference of opinion is made clear to both parties, each side will at least know exactly why they were angry and arguing in the first place.

Judy and Len were recently married. They both had successful careers in sales, were of the same religious and cultural background, had plenty of money and had come from stable homes. They had very little stress in their lives, but they were angrily arguing to the point of thinking about separation and divorce. Like many couples, they only came to counseling as a last ditch effort before splitting up. During our sessions, they learned to nurture their relationship and improve their communication skills. We were able then to hone in on their largest area of conflict.

Judy and Len had different ideas about how to spend their time after work. Judy had worked very hard as a student and was just beginning her career. Len had sowed his wild oats while still a student and jumped right into his career with easy success. Len believed that a couple should spend quiet evenings at home together. His job allowed him to come home about one hour before Judy. He had time to himself. Judy was experiencing a slower climb to success but still was feeling good about herself. She made friends at her job, some male, mostly female, almost all single. Her coworkers liked to go out after work for drinks and food. Judy was enjoying a social life with them she had not previously known. Len was jealous and threatened by his new wife's evenings out. Judy felt stifled and suffocated by Len, who was a more intense, verbal and emotional person. His anger made her feel that he was weak as a man and so made him less attractive to her. Len felt Judy was the "ice queen" and secretly questioned her commitment and fidelity. There were many heated discussions about how they spent their time after work.

As the counselor, I introduced no judgment about who was right or wrong despite the attempts by both Judy and Len to draw me into making this assessment. Some of you may be thinking that a married woman shouldn't have been out drinking with single friends. Len certainly felt that way. Others may be thinking that Judy is a free person and that Len was being immature. Judy certainly felt that way. What was important was not to provide them with a solution or take a side. This would have been rejected or sabotaged by the "loser" of the debate anyway. This couple needed help to develop the necessary skills to come up with their own mutual decision. Through communication skills training they came to see each other's feelings and points of view. Still, they simply disagreed with each other. They were also holding extreme positions. The more they had fought and the angrier they each had become, the more stubbornly they held to their positions and the more extreme these positions had become. In the controlled forum created by the counseling sessions and with communication tools, they became less angry and more able to see each other's positions and points of view. They still disagreed, but less heatedly.

However, Len and Judy said, "Okay we understand each other better, but we still don't agree. What do we do now?" We began to discuss negotiation skills or the making of contracts within a relationship. Some people react to this with, "But this isn't a business relationship, it is a marriage. We shouldn't have to make contracts." I disagree for many reasons. First, marriage is a formal contract. Many states give couples booklets when they go for their marriage licenses explaining that it is indeed a formal legal contract. Just try to dissolve a marriage and you will see how legal and complicated a contract it is. Second, these are skills, which although they seem rather artificial at first, are necessary given the level of conflict. Later, after they have mastered negotiating, a couple begins to incorporate contracts into the normal flow of the business of carrying out life together. Finally, an ongoing satisfying relationship does not just happen, it needs to be worked at.

One family therapy theorist has written that there are three types of implied contracts in any intimate relationship. One is a spoken and acknowledged contract. "I'll agree not to see anyone else if you agree, too." This is the start of a committed relationship. Another is an unspoken but acknowledged contract. *We do not cheat on each other* or *I'll put up with your unpleasant relatives and you will put up with mine.* The third is an unspoken, unacknowledged contract. These are on the more unconscious, deeply emotional level. *I'll meet your needs and you meet mine* or *I'll be the good father you never had and you will be the good mother I never had.*

There are two basic types of contracting techniques. One is the *quid pro quo. I do something for you; you do something for me.* "I'll make the dinner if you do the cleanup." "I'll walk your dog when you go on vacation if you pick up my newspaper deliveries when I go away." The other is compromise, when two people agree to meet somewhere near the middle. In Len and Judy's case, Len agreed not to give Judy an argument or make her feel guilty every time she came home late. Judy agreed to go out after work less often and spend more quiet evenings at home with Len. The focus was on frequency. Len needed to accept that Judy wanted some nights out. Judy needed to have fewer nights out and come home earlier when she did. He had felt these outings occurred too often. She had felt they were not often enough. In this type of contract each party must be willing to give up something. Len and Judy gave up their extreme positions and met somewhere near the halfway point. There is a balancing of some frustration of desires with some satisfaction of desires for both parties. When one is always getting their way, the other is building resentment. This is a toxic situation for any relationship. Each couple in a dispute must arrive at their own compromise, because compromising is necessary in any ongoing relationship. It worked for Len and Judy.

There are common areas of conflict in relationships. These can include:
- Finances
- How to raise and discipline children
- Involvement with extended families
- Cultural differences
- Religious differences
- How to use leisure time

:60 Second Exercise: Conflict Resolution

In the spaces provided list conflicts that are ongoing sources of frustration in your relationship or those you suspect may arise in the future.

Financial   _____

_____

_____

_____

_____

Raising Children   _____

_____

_____

_____

Involvement with   _____
Extended Families

_____

_____

_____

Cultural Differences   _____

_____

_____

_____

_____

Religious Differences   _____

_____

_____

_____

_____

Use of Leisure Time   _____

_____

_____

_____

_____

:60 Second Contract Exercise

In the space provided write down any informal contracts you have made with another person. Then write down some issues of conflict which have not been resolved with that person. After that, brainstorm some possible contracts either alone or with that other person. Brainstorm as many solutions as you can. Write them down. Then discuss these possible solutions with the other person and consider together the pros and cons of each. This will help the two of you arrive at an agreement. Next to each agreement check off what type it is: a *quid pro quo* or a compromise. Finally, once you have agreed upon a particular solution, do not rely simply on your verbal commitment. Write out your bargain in the form of a contract so that it is clearly and mutually understood. Both

parties should then sign the contract. Refer back to and review the contract in the following weeks to make sure each party is keeping his or her
end of the bargain. If this is not happening, do not get angry; simply
reaffirm or renegotiate the contract. Do not agree to things just to
appease the other person. This will only lead to resentment and a lack-
luster effort to stick to the contract. Try to arrive at compromises you
really can accept and live with. When you do something you would rather
not do or give up something you do not want to give up, keep your out-
look positive and your motivation up by reminding yourself of what you
are getting in return and how good it feels not to be embroiled in an
angry, ugly argument.

The pages following are here for you to write down existing informal
contracts, unresolved conflicts and potential solutions. Make copies and
use them. Once you have come to an agreement with your spouse or
partner, write out the agreement on the blank "contract" page at the end
of this chapter.

Existing Informal Contracts:

1) _____

_____

_____

_____

_____

2) _____

_____

_____

_____

_____

3) _____

_____

_____

_____

_____

4) _____

_____

_____

_____

_____

5) _____

_____

_____

_____

_____

Unresolved Conflicts:

1) _____

_____

_____

_____

_____

2) _____

_____

_____

_____

_____

3) _____

_____

_____

_____

_____

4) _____

_____

_____

_____

_____

5) _____

_____

_____

_____

_____

Brainstorming Solutions/Possible Contracts:

| | *Quid Pro Quo* | Compromise |
| | ☐ | ☐ |

1) _____

_____

_____

_____

_____

_____

| | *Quid Pro Quo* | Compromise |
| | ☐ | ☐ |

2) _____

_____

_____

_____

_____

_____

| | *Quid Pro Quo* | Compromise |
| | ☐ | ☐ |

3) _____

_____

_____

_____

_____

_____

            Quid Pro Quo Compromise
4) _____   ☐   ☐

_____

_____

_____

_____

_____

:60 SECOND CONTRACT

Quid Pro Quo ☐   Compromise ☐

_____

_____

_____

_____

_____

_____

_____

_____

_____

_____

_____

_____

_____

_____

_____

_____

_____

_____

_____

_____

_____

_____

_____

_____

_____

_____

Signed	**Signed**
Date	**Date**

:60 Second Tips: Conflict Negotiation

- Communication clarifies what an argument or conflict is really about.

- If communication leads to an impasse, negotiate a compromise.

- Formal contracts in a relationship are necessary.

- Contracts in a relationship may be spoken and acknowledged contracts, unspoken but acknowledged contracts, and unspoken, unacknowledged contracts.

- The *quid pro quo* and the compromise are two types of contracting techniques to use.

- Balance frustration and satisfaction for each party in a contract.

- Be aware you must give up something to get something.

- Identify your conflicts, brainstorm resolutions, note whether contracts are *quid pro quo* or compromise, write down and sign your contracts.

- Do not agree just to appease another. Arrive at compromises with which you really can accept and live.

CHAPTER 16

Anger, Substance Use and Abuse

"We deceive ourselves when we fancy that only weakness needs support. Strength needs it far more."
-Madame Swetchine

Substance use and substance abuse both have a large role to play in the destructive acting out of anger. Research has shown, for instance, that 65 percent of incidents of physical abuse in relationships have occurred when one or both of the participants are under the influence of either alcohol or drugs. Some substances like alcohol, marijuana and prescription tranquilizers or painkillers have what are known as disinhibiting effects. Just as they may reduce discomfort in social situations, they lower our natural controls making the acting out of anger much more likely. Other substances such as cocaine, speed and other stimulants can increase irritability and angry feelings. During withdrawal, irritability and anger can also be increased. For anger internalizers, food is often the substance of choice for soothing uncomfortable feelings in general and unexpressed anger in particular. Internalizers may also use and abuse other substances such as prescription tranquilizers to numb their anger. Side effects of some prescription medications come into play here, too. Relevant side effects can include agitation and irritability or decreased sexual drive which can lead to conflicts in personal relationships.

Take :60 Seconds to think about what over-the-counter, prescription or street drugs you are using and decide to look into whether they may be involved in your anger problems. Ask your pharmacist about side effects. Tell your medical doctors you are working on anger management, so they can modify your medications accordingly. They are not there to judge you, so it is okay to talk about your anger management work. Your efforts will reap greater results when you consider and alter the role of drugs and alcohol in your life.

There is an important distinction we need to look at now. This involves whether or not you are using substances in a problematic way. In other words, do you have a substance abuse problem? In my work with patients this is often a very sensitive and emotionally charged issue. Discussion is often met with defensiveness. Not only are they over-whelmed dealing with anger and legal, business or relationship problems, now they must examine another aspect of their lives that is causing them problems. They may also fear embarrassment and shame. They do not want to face the issue, because they often do not want or feel they are not able to give up the substance. Just as with anger control problems, there is a lot of denial about substance use and abuse.

Substance use is not a sign of weakness or a personal flaw. There are many reasons why people engage in this behavior. For some, there are genetic factors involved. A risk for substance abuse and addiction can be passed down from generation to generation. For others, it is a learned behavior. What you see your parents or friends doing as you grow up can shape your attitudes about the use of alcohol or drugs. The reasons behind your parents' or friends' use of these substances influences your reasons for using them. If your friends spend much of their time relax-ing at bars drinking cocktails, so may you. If your father used alcohol to cope with stress, you may follow his lead. If your mother popped pills to deal with frustration, you may use them to deal with the frustrations in your life. Once again, I must ask you to take an honest and courageous look inside yourself. I will be along for the journey. I will guide you in what must be done. There are many circumstances and many options to consider. Remember that even if you do not have a substance use or abuse problem, substances may still be involved in your anger problem. So do not skip to the next chapter. After we explore substance problems, we will also be looking at the role of non-problem use of substances in anger.

:60 Second Substance Abuse Screening Test #1

Answer the ten questions below—be honest!—by checking the "yes" or "no" boxes. Scoring instructions follow the test.

1. Do you feel you are a normal drinker or substance user? ☐ Yes ☐ No

2. Do friends or relatives think you are a normal drinker or substance user? ☐ Yes ☐ No

3. Have you ever attended a meeting of Alcoholics or Narcotics Anonymous (AA or NA)? ☐ Yes ☐ No

4. Have you ever lost friends, girlfriends/boyfriends or a spouse because of drinking or drug use? ☐ Yes ☐ No

5. Have you ever gotten into trouble because of drinking or drug use? ☐ Yes ☐ No

6. Have you ever neglected your obligations, your family or your work for two or more days in a row because of drinking or drug use? ☐ Yes ☐ No

7. Have you ever had severe shaking, heard voices or seen things that weren't there after heavy drinking or drug use? ☐ Yes ☐ No

8. Have you ever gone to anyone for help about your drinking or drug use? ☐ Yes ☐ No

9. Have you ever been in a hospital because of drinking or drug use? ☐ Yes ☐ No

10. Have you ever been arrested for driving while under the influence? ☐ Yes ☐ No

Scoring: For questions one and two give yourself 2 points for each "no" answer. On questions three, eight and nine give yourself 5 points for each "yes" answer. For all the remaining questions give yourself 2 points for each "yes" answer. Add all your points together. If your total score is 3 or less, your substance use should be non-problematic. A score of 4 points is suggestive of a drug abuse problem or alcoholism. A score of 5 points or higher indicates a strong likelihood that you have a serious drug or alcohol abuse problem.

:60 Second Substance Abuse Screening Test #2

The following is adapted from AA. It originally applied mainly to drinking and alcoholism, but I have modified it to include drug use and addiction. Remember, both drugs and alcohol are addictive substances.

Answer the questions honestly. There is no disgrace in having a problem and facing up to it. However, you do not have to share this with anyone; this test is for your personal use and information.

1. **Have you ever decided to stop drinking or using a substance for a week or so, but you were only able to abstain for a couple of days?**   ☐ Yes ☐ No

   Those who drink or take a substance to excess usually make all kinds of promises to stop or quit to themselves and their families. Most do not keep them.

2. **Do you wish people would mind their own business about your drinking or drug use and stop telling you what to do?**   ☐ Yes ☐ No

   If you are hearing about your problem from friends or family, you probably have one.

3. **Have you ever switched from one kind of drink or substance to another in the hope that this would keep you from getting drunk?**   ☐ Yes ☐ No

   Many people with alcohol or drug problems try all kinds of ways to not stop drinking or using drugs. They make their drinks weak.

Or, they just drink beer. They stop smoking pot and only take pills instead. Or, they only drink or do drugs on weekends. You name it, they have tried it. But if they drink *anything* with alcohol in it or do any kind of drug, they usually get drunk or high eventually.

**4. Have you had to have an "eye-opener" upon   ☐ Yes ☐ No
awakening during the past year?**
Do you need a drink or substance to get started or to stop shaking? This is a pretty sure sign that you are not simply drinking or using drugs "socially."

**5. Do you envy people who can drink or use   ☐ Yes ☐ No
prescription/street drugs without getting
into trouble?**
At one time or another, many substance abusers have wondered why they are not like most people who really can take it or leave it.

**6. Have you had problems connected with   ☐ Yes ☐ No
drinking or drug use during the past year?**
Be honest! Doctors say that if you have a problem with alcohol and keep on drinking, it will get worse—not better. If you are a drug user, much the same thing is true. Eventually, you will die or end up in an institution for the rest of your life. The only hope is to stop.

**7. Has your drinking or drug use caused   ☐ Yes ☐ No
trouble at home?**
Most people who drink or use drugs blame their problem on the people or conflicts at home. They do not see that their drinking or drug use has made everything worse and may have even caused the problems at home in the first place. Substance abuse never solves problems anywhere or anytime.

**8. Do you ever try to get "extra" drinks at a   ☐ Yes ☐ No
party because you do not get enough?
Or did you go home early to use?**

A lot of problem drinkers and drug users pop a few pills or have a "few" drinks before they go out for the evening just to get a head start. And if the partygoers aren't freely using drugs or the drinks aren't being served fast enough, the substance abuser leaves early to go someplace else where drug use is acceptable or alcohol is freely flowing.

9. **Do you tell yourself you can stop drinking**   ☐ Yes ☐ No
   or taking the substance anytime you want to,
   even though you keep using when you do
   not mean to?
   Many substance abusers kid themselves into thinking that they drink or do drugs when they want to, because they want to.

10. **Have you missed days of work/school**   ☐ Yes ☐ No
    because of alcohol or drugs?
    Many "call in sick" lots of times when the truth is that they are hungover, still high or too tired from being up all night binging.

11. **Do you have "blackouts"?**   ☐ Yes ☐ No
    A "blackout" is when a person has been drinking or using drugs and there are hours or days in which he or she cannot remember his or her actions. This is a pretty sure sign of alcoholic drinking or drug addicted behavior.

12. **Have you ever felt that your life would be**   ☐ Yes ☐ No
    better if you did not drink or take drugs?
    Many people who drink to excess or abuse drugs started out think-ing the substance made life seem better or more fun, at least for a while. After some time passed, however, they found they needed more and more of the substance to achieve the same high sensation and eventually, they needed the drugs just to function each day. They soon drink or do drugs to live and live to drink or do drugs.

What's your score?

Did you answer YES four or more times? If you did, you are likely in deep trouble with your drinking or drug use.

Now that you have taken the two screening tests, you probably have a good idea of how substance use or abuse fits into your life. However, sometimes there is still some doubt or uncertainty. In these cases, I have asked patients to stop using their preferred substances for ninety days. If the person can do it, there is probably no problem. If the patient is unable to give up the substance for that length of time, there is then more evidence that the client's substance use is out of control and may be abuse or dependence. If the problem is very serious, your doctor may want you to check yourself into a treatment center. For binge users, some can go for long periods without using. Then the person can lose a weekend or a week or two to substance use. If you binge, abstain longer than your usual period of sobriety.

It is not only recreational use of hard drugs which is a problem. If you are taking prescription medications under a doctor's care and are using them recreationally or more frequently than directed, you may be on the path to abuse or dependence, if you're not there already. If you think you do have a problem with your prescription medication, do not stop taking the medication. It could be very harmful to your health. Instead, discuss your suspected problem with your doctor (you will not get in trouble). He or she may have to wean you off your medication to avoid symptoms of withdrawal.

The basic answer to whether a person's use of a substance is at a level of abuse or dependence as opposed to normal consumption is simply whether the usage is causing a problem in his or her life. This can be a school, work, marital, family or legal problem. If there is still doubt, a look back at the family's history can help. Abuse and addiction have been linked to genetic factors. If there is a history of substance abuse in a person's family, it increases the person's risk for developing a substance abuse problem. If there is a possibility that you have a substance abuse problem, you must consider seeking further evaluation and treatment. You may need to work on the problem before or at least in tandem with your anger management work.

Initially, many people with substance abuse problems think that they will just stop on their own. I have seen that, just as with anger problems, unless a person gets professional help, the problem will usually continue. If you feel you may have a problem, an evaluation by a professional is needed. Where to go for this depends on your circumstances and the resources available where you live. In the next chapter we will discuss sources of help and how to find them.

When you arrive at an initial evaluation appointment, expect to complete some forms and questionnaires. Your confidentially will be maintained. Mental health professionals ask these questions, because they need to know background information to help them diagnose and treat your problem. In a face-to-face evaluation you will be asked more questions and given information by a therapist or counselor so that together you and the therapist can come to a decision on a need for intervention and a plan of action. It will be your decision as to what to do, but the professional will assist you in making any arrangements for treatment. At the end of the evaluation, the professional will make recommendations about which treatments will be needed. You may continue seeing a therapist for treatment itself or for guidance and support as you make your way through the steps to recovery from alcoholism or addiction.

There are a wide range of treatments for substance abuse and dependence problems. The type and extent of the problem and the substance(s) used will determine the type of treatment needed. "Substance abuse" exists when the use of a substance causes a problem in a person's life. "Substance dependence" is the same, but in addition there are signs of physiological addiction. This can include developing a tolerance, which is the need for more and more of the substance in order to produce the desired effect or "high." Upon discontinuing the substance, there will be withdrawal symptoms. Because of withdrawal, there may be a need for medical intervention such as hospitalization or close supervision by a doctor as the abuser's body is detoxified. As an individual is gradually weaned, she is put on another medication to reduce the risk of such dangerous withdrawal symptoms as seizures. Then she is weaned from that medication. This usually takes up to four or five days. Replacement medication will eliminate or lessen many of the unpleasant effects of withdrawal. Due to the dangers of unsupervised withdrawal, it is important not to stop using a drug (including alcohol) cold turkey without consulting a physician experienced in detoxification. This may be a psychiatrist or addictionologist. Your family doctor or local hospital emergency room is a good place to start.

Following "detox" there is sometimes a need for what is called rehabilitation. This may be needed when the problem is severe, when large amounts or a combination of many substances were being used or when the usage had been over a very long period of time. "Rehab" involves inpatient or residential treatment in which you stay at the facility full-time for weeks or months. The typical period is four weeks. During rehab you are provided a fully integrated treatment program. This can include medication evaluation and management, as well as attention to general medical needs and nutrition. Counseling and education are provided. Support groups are introduced. A discharge plan may include ongoing medication management by a psychiatrist, individual psychotherapy with a psychologist or clinical social worker and support group attendance. Inpatient rehab will be suggested when outpatient attempts to stop the substance abuse have failed. The least restrictive treatment is usually tried first. There are also outpatient intensive rehab programs that involve all of the components of inpatient programs except that you eat and sleep at home.

Less intensive treatment can include a combination of outpatient medication management, psychotherapy and support group attendance. This brings us to the importance of what are known as twelve-step support group programs. The first is Alcoholics Anonymous or AA. Narcotics Anonymous (NA) is very much the same, but for drug addicts. For people who abuse alcohol and drugs, a combination of AA and NA meetings are needed. There are other groups for gambling addicts (GA) and people with eating disorders (OA). Many addicts have other troubling issues in their lives and so may need to "work a program" on codependency (CODA) or one for adult children of alcoholics (ACOA). There are support groups for family members (Al Anon, Nar Anon, Al Ateen). These meetings are available in most towns at many convenient times. They are free. They stem from the discovery by two alcoholics that by helping others get clean and sober, one is also helped to stay clean and sober. Complete abstinence from alcohol and drugs "one day at a time" is the goal. The next two paragraphs are adopted from AA literature.

Is AA for you? Only you can decide whether you want to give AA a try—whether you think it can help you. We who are in AA came because we finally gave up trying to control our drinking. We still hated to admit that we could never drink safely. Then we heard from other AA members that we were sick. (We thought so for years!) We found out that many people suffered from the same feelings of guilt and loneliness and hopelessness that we did. We found out that we had these feelings because we had the disease of alcoholism.

AA does not promise to solve your life's problems. But we can show you how we are learning to live without drinking "one day at time." We stay away from that "first drink." If there is no first one, there cannot be a tenth one. And when we got rid of alcohol, we found that life became much more manageable.

AA and NA have helped millions of people to stay clean and sober. One needs to do more, however, than just go to meetings. One must get involved by choosing a sponsor. This person will guide you through the steps to recovery and will also be available to you for support. You need to also take people's phone numbers when they are offered. They will be offered to newcomers right away. You are to call someone any time you think you may want to use alcohol or narcotics. This person will talk you through it. Many of my patients have complained that AA or NA is not for them. I encourage people to give it a try, a commitment to attend for a good chunk of time. The program recommends ninety meetings in ninety days for the newcomer. I have also encouraged patients to try different meetings to find people with whom they can best relate. There are all types of people and all types of meetings, from smoking and non-smoking to all female or all male, among many others.

If you have even an inkling that you have a substance use problem, open the phonebook, pick up the telephone and find a professional to meet with to further evaluate it. A later chapter covers how to find help. Make an appointment and keep it. Do this now. Do not proceed with your anger management work until it is done.

Even if one does not have a substance abuse problem, alcohol and drugs still play a major role in anger problems. Therefore, make a :60 Second commitment to abstain from alcohol and drugs while you are using this book, performing the exercises and completing the assignments. You are to abstain throughout the entire period of working on anger management. In future situations, if you have been drinking or using drugs, be very careful when anger flares. Your newly found or strengthened anger management skills are self-control skills. Since controls are lowered while using substances, your skills will be weakened. These will be your times of greatest risk to relapse back to anger problems. Should a relapse occur, do not think you are back to square one, that all is lost. You have not lost all you have gained, but do not let yourself continue sliding back. Recommit and start over. Give yourself a new chance. In any process of change it is normal for there to be a few steps forward, some steps backward then some forward again. In the end your progress will continue steadily if you maintain your commitment and effort. Putting energy into guilt or self-recrimination serves no purpose. Use the energy to get moving forward again. Explain this to your partner to reduce his or her alarm should there be any backslides.

If you note that your anger relapses continue and always occur when you have been drinking or drugging, then you need to stop. The alcohol and drugs are perpetuating a major problem in your life. By definition they are a problem. Your efforts at anger management will be stalled. You stand to lose much more than the alcohol or the drug. Think about what you would rather lose. For example, your case of beer on the weekend or your marriage and daily contact with your children. Your drinking at lunch or your job. The *motivation* to stop anger problems and substance abuse is often what we stand to lose in our lives as a result of our drinking or drug habit. Use a :60 Second realization technique: Each time you pick up a drink or a drug, visualize what it may cost you in the bigger picture of your life.

Many people with addictions do not give them up until they "hit bottom." Each person has his or her own personal "bottom." This means that a person may have to lose almost everything before becoming motivated to stop. Some never hit bottom and do not stop. These are the people who lose their lives to their addiction. I remember a case I worked on while I was the Director of the New York City Police Department Alcohol Counseling Unit. One of the civilian employees had become increasingly confrontational with colleagues though she was with the Police Department for over thirty years. We discovered she was in "end stage alcoholism." This means that she was close to death as a result of her drinking. She was emaciated and all of her organs were failing. All eight of our Police Officer/Certified Alcohol Counselors worked with her over the course of a week. She was seen in our offices and visited at home and at her hangout/bar. She did not want to stop drinking and refused all help. She died soon after.

Be aware that there are many stereotypes of alcoholics and drug addicts. One common stereotype is that all addicts and alcoholics are street people. Many people use stereotypes to feed their denial of the problem. "I'm not an alcoholic. I'm not living in a cardboard box under the overpass." However, there are many functioning alcoholics or addicts. These people may be able to keep their jobs or their families despite their drinking or drugging. They have not lost everything yet, but their use of substances may be harming them and those close to them. Their family members and coworkers may even be helping to cover up the problem. "I won't let the boss know the reason you got so angry was that you were taking drugs again. I'll tell him you are sick." This is called enabling. Enablers think they are helping, but they are actually prolonging the problem. It is not until an addict has to face the consequences of his usage, that he may become motivated to stop. Nowadays, if a person is having trouble at his job because of alcohol or drug use, he is not fired; he is referred for help with his job contingent on his accepting the help.

If you have been drinking or drugging and feel anger cues, get yourself out of the situation; use a Time Out. If your partner is displaying anger and has been using drugs or alcohol, do not try to communicate. This serves no purpose. Walk away and wait till sober—and calmer—heads prevail.

:60 Second Alcohol/Drug Anger Log

Next you will find an Anger Log. Copy this and use it to keep a record of any alcohol or drug use on your part that occurs, what led up to it, what occurred during and what happened afterward. This is an "ABC" skill. It refers to Antecedents, Behaviors and Consequences. Through the log, you will be able to see any relationship between substance use and anger management difficulties. This will also help to identify what purposes the substances serve in your life. Some people use substances to lower anxiety in social situations, to fit in or to relax. Still others use them to block out unpleasant feelings. Some people just like the sensations they get from the substances they use. Once you discover the reasons for your substance use, brainstorm and then use alternatives to drinking or taking drugs. These may include finding other hobbies or things to enjoy, practicing relaxation skills, asserting yourself by saying NO, using stress management skills or finding an outlet for negative feelings.

Alcohol/Drug Anger Log

Date _____ Time _____ Location: _____

☐ Alcohol   ☐ Drug

List the substance(s) consumed:

_____ _____ _____

_____ _____ _____

How much? _____   Over how long? _____

What led up to using?_____

What happened or what did you experience during? _____

_____

_____

What happened afterwards? _____

_____

_____

What purpose did it serve? _____

_____

_____

What could you have done differently? _____

_____

_____

How did anger problems surface?_____

_____

_____

Do you recognize any patterns? _____

_____

_____

:60 Second Anger Internalizer Assignment

Many anger internalizers use substances, particularly food, to decrease the anger they hold inside and the resulting stress. **Complete the following log if you use food or other substances to "medicate" yourself so you will not be so angry.**

Date _____ Time _____ Location:_____

☐ Alcohol ☐ Drug ☐ Food

List the substance(s) consumed: _____

_____

Over what period of time?_____

What led up to it?_____

What happened or what did you experience during? _____

_____

_____

What happened afterwards? _____

_____

_____

What purpose did it serve? _____

_____

_____

What could you have done differently? _____

_____

_____

How did anger problems surface?_____

_____

_____

Do you recognize any patterns? _____

_____

_____

After reviewing these two assignments, return to previous sections for healthier replacements. For example, you may need to use relaxation or assertion skills to help you work through your anger without relying on drugs, alcohol or food.

:60 Second Tool

If either you or your partner has been using alcohol or drugs, do not attempt to communicate about a controversial issue. If anger cues are noticed, call an immediate Time Out. There can not be any effective or constructive communication when substances are in control.

:60 Second Exercise: Meaningful Sayings

Here is a list of AA slogans. They are brief summaries of very constructive ways to live one's life. Read through them and then rewrite those which you particularly like or those you feel are especially appropriate for you. Post this list in a spot you will see everyday, like your bathroom mirror.

1. Easy does it
2. First things first
3. Live and let live
4. Think...Think...Think
5. One day at a time
6. This too shall pass
7. If it works...Do not fix it
8. Keep coming back...It works if you work it
9. Stick with the winners
10. Identify, do not compare
11. Recovery is a journey, not a destination
12. Faith without work is dead
13. You are not required to like it, you are only required to do it
14. To thine own self be true
15. I came: I came to: I came to believe
16. Live in the now
17. Turn it over
18. Utilize, do not analyze
19. The elevator is broken, use the steps
20. We are only as sick as our secrets
21. There are no coincidences in the program
22. Be part of the solution, not the problem
23. Sponsors: Have one – Use one – Be one
24. I can't handle it, God; You take over
25. Keep an open mind
26. It works—It really does!
27. Willingness is the key
28. More will be revealed
29. You will intuitively know
30. You will be amazed

31. No pain…No gain
32. Go for it
33. Principles before personalities
34. Do it sober
35. Let it begin with me
36. Just for today
37. Pass it on
38. You either is or you ain't
39. Before you say "I can't," say "I'll try"
40. Do not quit five minutes before the miracle happens
41. Some of us are slicker then others
42. We're all there, because we're not all there
43. Addiction is an equal opportunity destroyer
44. Practice an attitude of gratitude
45. The road to recovery is a simple journey for confused people with a complicated disease
46. Live in the here and now
47. Have a good day unless you've made other plans
48. It takes time
49. 90 meetings, 90 days
50. You are not alone
51. Wherever you go, there you are
52. Make use of telephone therapy
53. Stay clean and sober for yourself
54. Look for similarities rather than differences
55. Live your life so you will never have to say "if only"
56. Remember that drug addiction is incurable, progressive and fatal
57. Try not to place conditions on your recovery
58. When all else fails, follow directions
59. Share your happiness
60. Respect the anonymity of others
61. Share your pain
62. Let go of old ideas
63. Try to replace guilt with gratitude
64. What goes around, comes around

65. Change is a process, not an event
66. Take the cotton out of your ears and put it in your mouth
67. Call your sponsor before, not after, you start using
68. Sick and tired of being sick and tired
69. Seven days without a meeting makes one weak
70. To keep it, you have to give it away
71. The price for serenity and sanity is self-sacrifice
72. Serenity = Reality = Inner peace and strength
73. Take what you can use and leave the rest
74. What if...
75. Yeah, but...
76. If only...
77. Help is only a phone call away
78. Around the program or in the program?
79. You can't give away what you do not have
80. Welcome and "keep coming back"
81. Anger is but one letter away from danger
82. Courage to change...
83. Easy does it, but do it
84. Bring the body and the mind will follow

My Favorites

1) _____

2) _____

3) _____

4) _____

5) _____

6) _____

7) _____

8) _____

60 Second Tips: Anger/Substance Use Connection

♦ Remember, substance use has a significant role in anger problems.

♦ Be aware that substances can disinhibit or weaken controls or cause increased irritability.

♦ Know that withdrawal and side effects can affect anger and relationships.

♦ Differentiate between substance use and substance abuse or dependence.

♦ Be aware that a family history of substance problems puts one at an increased risk for having a problem.

♦ Try to stop using for 90 days.

♦ Seek professional evaluation and assistance; you have a problem you cannot stop on your own.

♦ Choose from the wide range of treatments available.

♦ Abstain from alcohol and drugs while you are working on overcoming your anger problems.

♦ Be cognizant that substances can lead to anger problem relapses.

♦ Look for patterns in your substance use and anger problems.

♦ Use logs to learn the ABC's of your substance use.

♦ Learn the purposes substances serve for you.

♦ Find healthier replacements by reviewing earlier sections in this book.

CHAPTER 17

Calling in the Troops:
Seeking Professional Help

"Things do not change, we change."
-Henry David Thoreau

For many readers this manual will be sufficient to resolve anger difficulties. For some, extra help may be required. For example, if you cannot stick to the anger control techniques, if there is a substance abuse problem interfering or if a relationship partner is not cooperating, outside help may be needed.

Specialized treatment for anger management problems has only come about and proliferated over the last fifteen to twenty years. The earliest treatment was developed primarily for physical and emotional abuse. Later, treatments were generalized and adapted for anger management problems in general. Prior to this the problem was unacknowledged and, as a result, underestimated. If people did seek help, the stereotype of the silent psychoanalyst with a patient on a couch was pretty much all that was available. As with some other problems, psychoanalysis sometimes provided insights, but usually very little change. The problem was interpreted as being the result of sadomasochistic drives or instincts buried in individuals who welcomed abusive anger. This led to the position that victims brought about their own abuse and even wanted it, feeling so self-hateful that they believed they deserved to be punished and hurt. This fit with the past tendency in society to blame the victim.

Largely as a result of the women's movement there came a revolution in how anger problems have been understood and treated. The notion of victims wanting and bringing abuse upon themselves has been obliterated, and rightfully so. Many people have asked why victims would remain in situations or relationships where they are the continued objects of others' anger, domination and control. The question implies that the victim wants and even provokes the abuse. This may contribute to the faulty ideas held by many perpetrators that they were provoked and not responsible for their angry acting out, that the victims deserved what they got. The real answer to the question has to do with the domination and control that comes along with abuse. It has been realized that victims remain trapped in abusive relationships for many reasons. They are often cut off from financial resources and the support of friends and families, support which might help them out of their predicaments. Their self-esteem is torn down by the abuse they receive. They are told over and over that they are stupid, no good, unstable. This has an impact not unlike brainwashing. After repeatedly being told how terrible they are, victims begin to believe their abusers. They lose hope of leaving and ever being loved by others, for who could love the awful people they obviously are?

Think back to the story told earlier in the book about Dennis and his wife. The abuse in their marriage, like most with similar problems, was hidden behind closed doors. Society was less willing to intrude on the sanctity of their home. The fact that this has changed is reflected in laws requiring the mandatory reporting of child abuse and making child and marital abuse a crime. There are now mandatory arrest laws because of police reluctance to take action in domestic complaints and abuse. Dennis' abuse of his wife occurred behind closed doors. His wife's self-esteem was stripped away over a twelve-year period. She had no access to the resources to leave or demand change. As she became educated, she was empowered. Recall that the family knew nothing. Her first act was to let the cat out of the bag. She immediately received the support of Dennis' parents as well as her own. Her second step was to tell Dennis to leave. Their marriage would end if he did not get help. Dennis was no longer in control of his wife or his marriage. He realized he did not want to lose everything. He was ashamed and remorseful and he sought specialized help. Dennis and his wife are still together, happy and thriving, now that he has learned to control the anger that led to the abuse.

The first intervention developed to address abuse and aid victims was not a psychological one. What sprang up were numerous shelters where victims could seek refuge. They were given counseling and assistance in obtaining financial support and employment so that they could maintain independence. As the pendulum swung away from psychoanalysis and blaming the victim, there was a bias in the developing shelter movement. The belief was that all victims should remain completely independent and never return to any contact with the perpetrator. The view had changed from blaming the victim to totally blaming the perpetrator. Both were extremes and the latter proved impractical.

Shelter workers were becoming frustrated. The victims most often wanted to return to their relationships. They did not want the abuse, but they did not want to lose the love, their marriages, nor cut off their children's other parent. If we consider parental rights in divorce, we see that a complete cutoff is not practical nor is it usually in the best interest of the children involved. With no-fault divorce and shared custody, relationships continue as long as there are minor children.

Those in the shelter movement realized that they had to adjust their goals. They then turned to psychology for assistance. There needed to be a place where perpetrators and victims could receive treatment of a new kind. Psychologists responded by developing programs of an entirely different approach than had been used by psychoanalysts. It was fortunate that at the time psychology had gone through its own revolution and there were new therapies and approaches that were based on learning. No longer did we need to rely solely on theories of inner instincts and drives and passive insight-oriented techniques. We had a new arsenal of other interventions aimed at retraining behavior and thinking.

Specialty clinics sprang up as quickly as had the shelters. These clinics still exist and serve a crucial purpose as a first step to change. I was fortunate to be involved in one of those early clinics. Dr. Alan Rosenbaum was my mentor and he developed one of the new intervention programs. We attended conferences and networked with other

programs to share ideas. We conducted research to further our understanding of the problems and to hone in on the most effective treatment interventions. We presented and published our results to inform
other investigators and treatment providers. The education I received
from Dr. Rosenbaum through this process has served and enriched my
entire career.

I will never forget the response I received while seeking subjects for
my doctoral research. I approached seven major family violence clinics
in and around the New York City area. Everyone welcomed me with
open arms. These treatment providers were excited to see that someone
from a university was interested in the problem. Later they began refer-
ring their workshop graduates to me for individual and marital therapy
follow-up. Without them I would not have been able to establish myself
as a young private practitioner in the very competitive New York City
area.

There are now specialty clinics in almost every county in every state
across the United States. Many are state funded and are part of community mental health centers or abuse shelters. Others are research grant
supported and are part of university clinics. The Salvation Army has
used a portion of its contributions to run clinics as well.

With changes in our society and the recognition of the range of
anger problems, the clinics have expanded their focus from relationship
abuse to the treatment of anger in general. The first such societal change
involves the vast increase of violence in the workplace. More recently, we
have seen a proliferation of violence among teens in our schools (I will
be writing about teens managing their anger in my next book) and now
we are seeing anger generated by the sudden acceleration of terrorism.
With those events, psychology has responded and there are both specialists and clinics which can help you learn to deal with anger. Expertise
and methods have been applied more generally in what are now considered "Anger Management or Anger Alternative Programs." The treatments have also spread to other settings where anger problems manifest
themselves. Many companies have workplace violence policies, prevention procedures and employee assistance programs. Many schools have
established their own mental health centers and educational prevention

programs. Crisis intervention specialists can help you deal with cata-strophic stress and anger. Assistance is more and more widely available and accessible.

Let's take a closer look at more intensive treatment; what to expect and how to find it.

A therapist or counselor...

- Seeks information from you through questions, tests or written logs.
- Provides information or education.
- Clarifies issues or problems.
- Offers a new perspective.
- Disputes faulty ideas.
- Reinforces positive behaviors.
- Focuses and guides your efforts.
- Keeps you on track in your efforts.
- Teaches new skills.
- Supports you in your efforts.
- Guards your autonomy so that you do not become dependent on the therapy.
- Weans you from therapy at the appropriate time.

A therapist can tailor an approach to your specific situation and needs in the area of anger. Where this manual is somewhat generic to help the greatest number of people possible, therapy is individualized. However, your therapy will benefit greatly from your use of this book. It should go more quickly and your therapist will appreciate your contribu-tion as a knowledgeable and active partner in the process of change. You'll find that both group and individual therapy are available. Each has its pros and cons. Groups give you exposure to others like yourself. All of the members benefit from hearing each other's stories. Everyone learns more. If you are not comfortable with group therapy, there is indi-vidual or one-on-one counseling. You get more attention from the coun-selor and treatment is tailored just for you.

Remember not to act discouraged. Therapy is working if it is diffi-cult. It takes joint effort by the therapist and the patient. Many patients come to a point where they show that they begin thinking like the therapist. "Hey, Doc, this week I was in a tense situation and I thought about what you would say. I thought I might call you, but I handled it myself." This is a sign that therapy has been successful and the patient is coming to the end of the individual phase of treatment. Remember, in anger management there first needs to be treatment of the anger in individual or group therapy. Only after the anger is under control is it safe to move on to working out other problems, like relationship issues. Then you can attend therapy with your partner to resolve your long-standing conflicts and learn new relationship skills.

So anger therapy is not for "crazy" people. I see everyday people with jobs, families, friends and hobbies. These are people who are having problems in living and need assistance to overcome them. Therapy is not a stamp of weakness or a sign of a flawed character. It is a healthy endeavor. When I evaluated candidates for employment as law enforcement officers, they were often reluctant to admit to having been in therapy. They were unaware that the evaluating psychologist and the department were happy that they had been in therapy. This was considered a good thing. If they were to have problems once hired, they would be likely to seek appropriate treatment. This openness is viewed as a positive. No one was rejected for having been in therapy.

There is much confusion about the difference between psychiatrists and psychologists. Historically, psychiatrists practiced therapy mostly of the Freudian or psychoanalytic type. In the old days this was pretty much the only kind of therapy available. It was expensive and time-consuming. A patient was seen for an hour a day, five days a week. He or she lay on a couch with the analyst sitting behind. This was so that the analyst did not interrupt the patient's flow of free associations (Although Freud has said that this was also for his own comfort, since he could not tolerate having patients looking at him all day.). The patient was asked to say whatever came to mind. Every few weeks or so the analyst offered an interpretation or a restating of what the patient was saying in the framework of the analyst's theory. The analyst was inactive, because it was felt that it was better for the patient to figure out his or her own behavior, thoughts or emotions. This type of therapy is mainly for those who are interested in exploring and understanding themselves, for gaining insight into themselves. You might pursue it if you are so inclined, but only after you deal with your specific problem—anger. Psychoanalytic therapy is not effective in treating this problem.

Today some psychiatrists primarily prescribe medications which have been found to help such problems as anxiety, depression and mood swings, as well as obsessions and compulsions, among others. They treat symptoms from a medical or biological point of view. Psychologists are doctoral level professionals who do psychological testing and conduct psychotherapy. They do not prescribe medication. After an evaluation they may refer you to a psychiatrist for medication. You might continue weekly psychotherapy with the psychologist and see the psychiatrist monthly for fifteen minute medication management appointments. For problems where medication is necessary, the research has shown that medication and therapy together are more effective than either one alone. In addition to Licensed Psychologists, Licensed Clinical Social Workers and in many states other masters level professionals such as Licensed Mental Health Counselors and Licensed Marriage and Family Therapists provide psychotherapy. You can probably tell by the word "licensed" that the states do quality control to ensure that the public is treated only by people who are properly educated and trained. Always seek help from a licensed professional, unless you are being seen at a specialized clinic or treatment program certified by the state. Such programs also have to meet certain standards, but the professionals working there are not necessarily licensed themselves.

In seeking treatment for anger, look for someone who is experienced in or specializes in treating anger management problems. Do not be afraid to ask to speak to the therapist about his or her experience and approach. If you call a clinic, you will often get an appointment scheduler on the phone. Ask to speak to an intake worker or therapist on staff. Find out if he or she specializes in anger management and how he or she approaches the treatment of anger at the clinic. Basically, you are looking for someone who has an active practice in that area, intervenes frequently after listening, provides education and assigns homework. Specialists will also know that treatment needs to begin with a focus on the anger in individual therapy. Unless you have completed an anger management workshop or have used this book successfully, an experienced therapist would not recommend your starting in joint marital therapy or relationship counseling.

If you have health insurance you can see a private psychologist. Therapy is a covered benefit. Since many insurance plans are now HMOs and PPOs, you can call the plans and ask for names from their lists of providers in your area. Ask for referrals to psychologists who specialize in treating your problem, whether it be lack of anger control or substance abuse. When you call to make an appointment, remember to ask to speak briefly with the psychologist. In addition to finding out about his or her background and relevant experience, you can see if the therapist's manner makes you feel comfortable.

Another resource is your family doctor. Ask the doctor for a referral to a mental health specialist. Your company may have an employee assistance program. There may be a professional there who can evaluate your needs. If not, a referral can be made. Employee assistance counselors will respect your confidentiality within the company since you are voluntarily contacting them for help. They are excellent referral sources since they have already screened professionals in the area, have referred to them before and have solicited feedback about them. Some corporate employee assistance programs will pay for an evaluation and several initial sessions.

If there is a local teaching hospital, call there for a referral. The hospital may have an outpatient clinic itself. A local university with a psychology department will also have a treatment clinic. Most counties have addiction treatment or mental health treatment centers. These operate on a sliding scale basis, meaning that you are charged fees based on your income and family size. These are always less expensive than private practitioners. Look in the Yellow Pages of your telephone book under the name of your county. There are other sliding scale organizations such as family service agencies, Catholic Family Services or Jewish Family Services, for example. These will be listed in the telephone book in the white pages by name. If you are a member of a house of worship, referrals should also be available from your religious leader. Most counties will also have a mental health association. For example, where I live, in a suburb of Fort Lauderdale, we have the Mental Health Association of Broward County. This is an excellent resource for referrals of all types. The number is available through information or the white pages.

There are several major, national organizations that can provide information, assistance or referrals. One, the National Mental Health Association can be reached by calling their toll-free number: **(800) 969-NMHA** or you can visit their Web site: **www.nmha.org**. They can give you the telephone number for your local association. Another, the National Domestic Violence Hotline, is a very good source for referrals about anger problems. Their toll-free telephone number is **(800) 799-SAFE** and their Web site is **www.ndvh.org**. This is a non-profit organization that is a clearinghouse for information on help available for anger problems. All practitioners and programs have submitted lengthy applications and letters of recommendation to ensure their competence and the relevancy of their experience. This hotline can direct you to clinic programs or private practitioners near you. The American Red Cross is another national organization that provides counselors and referrals to help people suffering from stress and anger problems following catastrophic events. The toll-free number is **(866) GET-INFO** and their Web site is **www.redcross.org**.

Take :60 Seconds to think about stigma again. Please do not be put off by the words domestic violence. You do not have to be violent to need help or to seek help from an agency that specializes in treating "spouse abuse." The people who work in the agencies usually have good experience in treating anger control problems in general. Many anger control workshops and programs are run out of these agencies because historically they were the first groups which specifically dealt with anger problems. Today the treatment has been generalized to address all aspects and levels of anger control problems.

If you find yourself thinking:

·   *I wouldn't call there.*
·   *I would not go to one of those places.*
·   *I do not beat my wife.*
·   *I'm not going to be associated with a bunch of batterers.*

Replace those thoughts with:

- *There are no logical reasons why I would not call anyone who could help.*
- *Like me, a wife beater has an anger management problem.*
- *I do not mind being associated with anyone who has a problem and is doing something about it.*

With regard to stigma it is important to note that professionals have an ethical responsibility to protect your confidentiality. In fact there are numerous rules for keeping information private. These rules are also mandated by law and should be explained to you at the outset of an initial appointment. There are some legally mandated instances in which confidentiality cannot be maintained. Essentially, the mental health or substance abuse professional is legally mandated to report any instance of abuse of a child, a senior citizen or a disabled individual. They also must take action to prevent you from acting on direct suicidal and homicidal intentions and specific plans to carry those out. Except for these instances, everything you say is kept between you and the professional.

You have a right to see your records. The professional may provide you with the full record, a summary or may want to go over it with you in person to explain the notes and answer your questions.

Your records can only be released with your written consent. If you introduce your own emotional state in any legal action you take or are involved in, then the other party may be able to get your records. This would be through a court order signed by a judge after hearing arguments by all legal counsel. Most of these situations will not apply to the vast majority of you. Also realize that in any court, the fact that you sought help would be seen as a positive thing. For example, in divorce, most judges require psychotherapy before legal action can proceed.

Rest assured that there are many safeguards to protect your privacy. Many clinics and private practitioners are set up with sensitivity to your privacy in mind. That is why you may see chiropractic, dental, podiatry and optometry offices in just about every shopping center, but not psychology or psychiatry offices. You probably have never seen a psychology office next to everyone's favorite bakery, pharmacy, dry cleaner or video rental store. You will not be running into your next door neighbor as she exits the supermarket and you enter the office with the big, neon "Mental Health" sign above it.

Most importantly, if you or someone else feels you need therapy for anger management, be open to it. Just as you picked up this book, pick up the phone and make some calls. Be patient in finding the right place or person and in waiting for an appointment. Give the treatment a real try. If you want to quit after one session, do not. Tell the therapist about it. The therapist will help sort out what the problem is and make adjustments or refer you to someone else if you are not comfortable. Do not be afraid of hurting the therapist's feelings. They are there to listen to you and be sure that you receive the best help for your needs. Therapists know that all people do not click with every therapist. Be patient and stick with it. You are worth the effort. Remember, bring the mind so that the body will follow.

:60 Second Tips: Final Thoughts on Anger Management

♦ There are specialized interventions for anger management problems.

♦ If you need further treatment, see a therapist.

♦ Ask the therapist about his or her experience and approach.

♦ Treatment can be tailored for your specific situation and needs.

♦ Treatment has been generalized from an early focus on domestic violence to now include violence in the workplace and in the schools and to anger problems in general, not necessarily of the violent type.

♦ Therapy will be much like your use of this book except that it will be more specific to your personal circumstances and characteristics.

♦ Therapy is successful when you become your own good therapist.

♦ It is not for "crazy" people.

♦ The therapist will refer you for medication if needed.

♦ There are many resources for receiving an informed referral.
  The National Mental Health Association (800) 969-NMHA
  The National Domestic Violence Hotline (800) 799-SAFE

♦ Your treatment is private and confidential.

♦ Bring the mind so that the body will follow.

EPILOGUE

"You must be the change you wish to make in the world."
-Mahatma Gandhi

This book began with a general overview about anger and anger management. I indicated that adults frequently engage in what is termed over-controlled hostility. They have strong controls against the expression of anger. We learned that anger builds and builds in such cases, until some relatively minor events trigger intense, explosive outbursts of anger. The duration of these "explosions" is usually short and the individuals often experience guilt and remorse afterward.

Under-controlled hostility, we learned, occurs when an individual has few controls against the expression of anger. This person's angry outbursts are more frequent but less intense. They may be directed at any number of objects, including friends, bosses, teachers, strangers, spouses, loved ones and even the police.

Methods of treating anger need to be tailored to the sub-type of hostility displayed, although it must be noted that the over-controlled versus under-controlled distinction is not absolute. There is a blending across age populations and even within individuals. In my desire to teach techniques for the appropriate releasing and expression of anger, all aspects of hostility were covered and all techniques were presented.

I also noted that adults have been known to have been under the influence of alcohol or other substances in about 50 percent of the cases where anger has been expressed in a destructive way. Substance abuse is an issue that needs to be addressed, perhaps professionally.

Another important distinction I made is that women are equally as likely as men to express anger in destructive ways. With regard to relationship violence, there may be fewer reports of female violence toward males, because of the stigma for men in identifying themselves as victims of physical abuse. I tried to dispel this stigma, because of the importance for men to learn to walk away when provoked either verbally or physically. Another reason men often do not make official reports against women may be that the physical damage caused by women is usually not as severe as that caused by men. However, the emotional damage can be more painful and longer lasting than any physical damage. Research has shown that women frequently are more verbally facile than men and often have the upper hand in arguments. Men may then frustratedly turn to expressions of physical power to regain control. I believe I presented in the book an equal weighting of cases involving male and female expressions of anger.

The ultimate goal has been for anger to be expressed in a non-threatening, calm, verbal manner. The person who earlier felt out-of-control anger should now be able to say "I feel angry. I feel that way because…" Remember the first lesson of anger management: anger is a normal emotion and everyone experiences it. In fact, there is a popular psychological test which presents the true/false statement "Sometimes I feel so angry I could throw or break something." This test is often used to evaluate candidates for public safety positions and people invariable respond "False" to that statement, thinking it is the preferred answer. Instead, it contributes to increasing their "Lie Scale," which is the test's built-in indicator of how openly and honestly the candidate is responding. It is perfectly natural for people sometimes to feel so angry they want to throw or break something. Note, however, that the statement does not imply that a person has *actually* thrown or broken something in anger, but that the idea has come to mind although not acted upon.

I pointed out that the distinction between expressing anger in words as opposed to acting out on anger is an important one. People are encouraged to realize that calmly stating "I feel angry right now because…" is an example of expressing anger in words and is a constructive, positive way to express their feelings. Another point made is that cursing, shouting and verbal put-downs are not constructive and are poor methods of acting on anger, as is any sort of physical aggression, including slamming doors, throwing or breaking objects, pushing, grabbing, slapping or hitting. We are not wrong for feeling anger, but going about expressing it the wrong way can get us into trouble.

Hopefully, if the techniques in this book are utilized, the emotion of anger will be normalized. As is true of all our emotions, whether glad, sad, scared or mad, anger probably had survival value for our species. Recall that the adrenaline rush, the tunneling of vision, the rapidity of heartbeat and the flow of blood to the extremities undoubtedly made us better hunters, runners or fighters. For the most part in modern society, however, this "fight or flight" response is not often needed. However, as I explained, unexpressed anger has been related to the development of ulcers, headaches, back and neck pain, anxiety, panic disorders and depression. Many angry acts are now illegal. They are destructive to others and ultimately to the self. Knowing the down side of angry acts has been, I hope, one of the motivators for change.

There are several short, psychological, paper-and-pencil inventories which I drew upon to create a self-test for problematic anger expression. Readers who took the test at the beginning of their anger work should use it as a baseline against which to measure progress as they go along practicing and using the anger management techniques.

I made the point that an individual is not bad, sick or crazy for having an anger management problem. It is the behavior that is unacceptable and destructive to the individual. Most anger problems are learned and can be unlearned. Fifty percent of physically abusive individuals either experienced or witnessed physical abuse as they were growing up. The acting out of anger in a verbally or physically abusive manner became an acceptable method to them. Through modeling, they learned to use it themselves. Some people who grow up in households where parents stifle their expressions of anger by being punitive or abusive, tend to become over-controlled in their experience and expression of anger. Others who grow up in broken or chaotic families where there are few rules and limits but much acting out of anger, tend to become under-controlled in their expression of anger. There are reasons why people come to have problems with anger. They are not simply "bad people."

As I have extensive experience not only in research but also in treating anger management problems in my practice, I drew upon a wide range of actual case histories to make the reading less abstract and more useful for the reader. Through this real-world experience with my patients, I attempted to explain the concepts and techniques of anger management in everyday terms.

You have now learned that anger is a normal emotion which we all feel at times. The ultimate goal is to successfully manage anger by expressing it in non-threatening words and tone of voice. For instance, simply say, "I feel angry. I feel that way because…" This is a constructive, non-damaging way of expressing anger, one which will be much more likely to be heard and responded to in a positive way. Expressing your anger in this manner will become self-reinforcing, because any behavior that is rewarded tends to be repeated.

By utilizing the quizzes, exercises and worksheets in this book, I hope you now understand a great deal more about what triggers anger, yours or that of someone close to you. If you felt out-of-control in expressing your anger, I hope you have learned the *:60 Second Anger Management* techniques that work best for *you* and that you practice these skills everyday. When managing anger becomes second nature, feelings of self-worth and self-esteem will blossom and grow, improving relationships in every aspect of life.

On the opposite page is a distillation of the anger management skills I have tried to impart in this book.

:60 Second Lifelong Guidelines

♦ Identify your personal signals and cues that tell you you are feeling anger.

♦ Tune into physical sensations to tune into your emotions.

♦ Call a Time Out when you notice anger cues; stick to the Time Out rules.

♦ Journal to express and learn about your anger.

♦ Break the feeling, thinking, acting out cycle of anger by relaxing.

♦ Relax on cue in :60 Seconds by practicing the techniques often.

♦ Control what you think or say to yourself; choose positive thoughts.

♦ Focus on the constructive; dispute your irrational thoughts.

♦ Think preferences, not *shoulds, oughts* or *musts*.

♦ Master your worry.

♦ Distract yourself from angry thoughts.

♦ Replace negative thoughts about yourself with positive ones.

♦ Assert yourself by expressing anger calmly and in words.

♦ Sidestep unnecessary power struggles; don't debate who is right and who is wrong.

♦ Express yourself in "I feel…" statements, not "I think…" statements.

♦ Say "I feel angry because…. I would like…."

♦ Work on responding with a simple "No."

♦ Address one issue at a time when disagreements or anger arise.

♦ Use anger as a cue to look deeper inside yourself; risk expressing deep feelings.

♦ Utilize the "Holding the Floor" and Paraphrasing techniques in arguments with others.

♦ List three things you can do to make a situation better; post it in a prominent place.

♦ Identify conflicts, brainstorm resolutions and use the Contract technique.

♦ Write down and sign your contracts; note whether they are *quid pro quo* or compromises.

:60 Second Lifelong Guidelines *(cont.)*

♦ Identify patterns of substance abuse in your anger management problems.

♦ Learn the purpose substances serve for you; look for healthier replacements.

♦ Seek professional help if you cannot stop using a substance for ninety days.

♦ Know that you can manage your anger in a healthy fashion by incorporating these positive actions in your life.

Now is the time for some post-*:60 Second Anger Management* testing. Return to the two anger management tests in chapter 3. Use these now to check on your progress. Pick up this book again in three months and review it, using the tests to again check on your progress. Do the same thing in another three months. In time you should see improvements in your ability to express your anger in non-violent, non-aggressive ways. Be vigilant and faithful in utilizing the system of anger management I have provided. Remember: Bring the mind so that the body will follow.

Other Titles in the :60 Second Series

(In print in 8 countries: China, Holland, Germany, Romania, Russia, Turkey, United Kingdom, United States)

:60 Second Chronic Pain Relief: The Quickest Way to Soften the Throb, Cool the Burn, Ease the Ache
by Dr. Peter G. Lehndorff with Brian Tarcy ★ ISBN: 0-88282-151-2 (pb), $13.95
"Provides information that can be digested and put to use quickly and easily." -- *Sentinel & Enterprise*
"Goes beyond most pain titles in providing simple remedies." -- *Bookwatch*

:60 Second Menopause Management: The Quickest Ways to Handle Problems and Discomfort
by Carol R. Schulz and Mary Jenkins, M.D. ★ ISBN: 0-88282-137-7 (pb), $13.95
"If you're too busy to think about menopause but are
feeling its symptoms, this may be the book for you." -- *New York Newsday*

:60 Second Mind/Body Rejuvenation: Quick Tips to Achieve Inner Peace and Body Fitness
by Curtis Turchin, DC, MA ★ ISBN: 0-88282-181-4 (pb), $14.95
- Rodale Book Club and *Prevention* Book Club Selection
"Well-written, easy-to-understand...a bright light illuminating
a path to a better, fitter life...sound, common sense advice." -- *Metaphysical News*
"Leads to stress and pain relief, comfort, emotional well-being [and] spiritual enhancement." -- *Today's Books*

:60 Second Sleep-Ease: Quick Tips for Getting a Good Night's Rest
by Shawn Currie, Ph.D. and Keith Wilson, Ph.D. ★ ISBN: 0-88282-212-8 (pb), $13.95
"Medically sound...help[s] with the problems of insomnia that are so prevalent in society." -- *www.newbookreviews.com*
"Exceptional. [The authors] offer ways to efficient, quality night's sleep." -- *Today's Books*

:60 Second Stress Management: The Quickest Way to Relax and Ease Anxiety
by Dr. Andrew Goliszek ★ ISBN: 0-88282-115-6 (pb), $14.95
- Doubleday Book Club and Rodale Book Club Selection
"Highly recommended." -- Library Journal
"A well-researched book... An important acquisition to any academic or public library." -- *Choice*

To order any titles or to receive a catalog please call New Horizon Press toll-free at (800) 533-7978 or visit our web site: www.newhorizonpressbooks.com. To mail your order, please fill out the coupon below and send with check or money order to New Horizon Press, P.O. Box 669, Far Hills, NJ 07931.

Qty.	Title	Unit Price	Total Price
_____	_____	$_____	$_____
_____	_____	$_____	$_____
_____	_____	$_____	$_____
_____	_____	$_____	$_____
	*NJ Residents only, please add applicable sales tax.	Subtotal:	$_____
	**Shipping within Continental U.S. is $4.00 each book, $0.50 each	*Sales Tax (NJ Only):	$_____
	additional book. For Canadian or foreign orders, call for shipping costs.	**Shipping:	$_____
	Please allow 3 to 4 weeks for delivery.	**TOTAL:**	$_____

Bill To:
Name: _____
Company: _____
Street: _____
City: _____
State: _____ Zip: _____
Tel. No.: _____

Ship To:
Name: _____
Company: _____
Street: _____
City: _____
State: _____ Zip: _____
Tel. No.: _____

★★*Order any two (or more) titles to receive a 20% discount*★★